Praise for *The No-Fluff Business* and Sarah Mae Ives

"Building my own business is something that completely transformed my life —I now know what's possible and it's available to us all, which is why Sarah's book is a must-read. Not only is her story super inspiring, but she also teaches you how you can do it too, so you can make money doing what you love, make a difference in this world and live life on your terms."

Carrie Green, Founder and CEO of the Female Entrepreneur Association (FEA), author of the international bestseller, *She Means Business*, and an accomplished public speaker.

"Sarah's ability to be both kind and warm AND no-nonsense is truly a unique combination of characteristics that lend themselves beautifully to being able to teach you how to be a successful online entrepreneur. I'm astounded at how witty her delivery is, and how straightforward her tools and techniques are. She truly has a unique perspective of how to cut down time frames and create a lucrative income from your sofa in your pjs. This is a MUST-READ!"

Abi Levine, Divine Money Manifestation Coach
Founder of Millionaire Mindset Mastery

"Sarah's story and her no-fluff approach in *The No-Fluff Business* are about someone who has accomplished what women with big dreams working from home online want to accomplish—she doesn't just dream; she punches through adversity and makes it happen!
I have been personally inspired by Sarah's journey, her growth, and her style of making the seemingly impossible completely accessible for anyone who wants to listen, grow, and take action. If you're ready to shift up your life in a transformational way, Sarah is your go-to guide and mentor."

Jessica Mae, Visionary of The Bottom Line®

"Sarah's inspiring, yet no-nonsense approach will help you cultivate the most critical aspects of starting a successful business without the fluff. Sarah's unique vantage point from being "behind the scenes" of so many businesses (including mine!) through her years in advertising gives her a unique advantage at identifying the trouble spots so many new entrepreneurs find themselves in.

In this highly relatable book, you'll get the wisdom you need to crush it in business and life."

Monick Halm, expert, educator and advocate
Founder of Real Estate Investor Goddesses

"Starting a business can feel overwhelming and confusing. It's easy to get lost in the online business vortex of ideas...Sarah candidly talks about how to navigate these difficulties in an easy to understand and practical way."

Scott Oldford, Business Mentor, Investor, and Advisor and Creator of The Relevancy, Omnipresence and Intimacy Marketing & Sales Method, 6 Pillar Framework, and REwired.

The No-Fluff Business

The 90-Day Guide to More Money, Freedom, and Purpose Online

Sarah Mae Ives

The No-Fluff Business
The 90-Day Guide to More Money, Freedom, and Purpose Online

ISBN-13: 978-1-7779732-0-9

SARAH Mae IVES
TO LEARN MORE...
join the FREE training:
How I Built A $10,000
Per Month At-Home
Business While The
Kids Were At School
https://watch.sarahmae
ives.com/10kmonths

DEDICATION

This book is dedicated to all the women who want more freedom and control over their lives. For the women who want to contribute to the world with purpose and be rewarded proportionately. This book is also dedicated to my father, Gerry Daley, who showed me, through example, the type of tenacity, commitment and drive that it takes to succeed as an entrepreneur.

FOREWORD

"ROI? Is that a store that sells fleeces?" was an actual thought my former self had.

I went from covering business news for a decade as a financial reporter and anchor on CNN, CNBC and Bloomberg, to trying to be in business for myself when I saw a need for accessible financial guidance for women. All of a sudden, I went from interviewing CEOs and moguls to wanting to be like them. Except… I didn't know how. I mean, I couldn't even talk the talk, so how in the world would I be able to walk the walk?

I didn't learn anything about money or business in school. The truth is: none of us do. And even if we do go to b-school, study economics or happen to have a dad who helped us decode *The Wall Street Journal* around the breakfast nook, the world of business changes. Every. Damn. Day.

What I learned—in the school of Hard Knocks—is that as soon as you think you have something figured out…boom! Another obstacle to get around. Another lesson to learn. Another round of business owner whack-a-mole to play.

But (yes, there *is* always a but), knowledge isn't power. Action is power. You have a whole internet of business information at your fingertips, and likely you still feel clueless. That's understandable. Sometimes too much information can be overwhelming and lead to inaction.

In *The No-Fluff Business,* Sarah Mae Ives gives you what you need to know minus, well, the fluff. She demystifies what it's really like to start an online business. She tells you exactly what you actually need to know if you want to follow her footsteps and start a 7-figure online business yourself. She basically helps you skip the hard steps she had to take, and gives you the cheat code that took her years to figure out. Lucky you…those are all the things I *wish* I had had when I started in business but didn't.

Here's a secret about business I learned the hard way: it's not that complicated. It's really just some jargon to learn and some acronyms to flesh out. And while any language sounds intimidating before you can speak it, I know you've figured out harder things in life.

The truth is: you don't need to know everything about finance or business. There is no test about economic theories or the history of Wall Street. You just need to know the stuff that applies to *you* and *your* goals.

Sarah helps you do the two most important things to start your own business: figure out what makes a good business idea, and how to make money from it online. It's definitely simple, but not easy. So, if you want to explore being in business for yourself, my dear, today (and the next 89) is as good a day as any. I promise, if I—who started as a poetry major in college—can have a multi-million-dollar company and be living a bigger life in business than I ever could have imagined, then so can you.

Oh, and P.S.: ROI, if you don't already know, stands for "Return on Investment." I believe the biggest ROI you can get in your life and career doesn't come from the stock market (breaking news from a finance expert I know)! It comes from you. The greatest return you can make comes from investments—like this book and the actions you take from it— that you make in yourself.

Nicole Lapin

#1 NYT Bestselling Author, Money Expert and Speaker

TABLE OF CONTENTS

INTRODUCTION

CHAPTER 1

LET'S BREAK SOME RULES

"Sarah, you are not normal."

I was a 27-year-old single mom with a master's degree and a "good" research job at a hospital in Ottawa. I commuted an hour in traffic every day. I liked the patients I worked with and felt close to a couple of my co-workers. I had an old house, a huge mortgage, and $33,000 of debt. At the time, it didn't seem much different from what everyone else was doing. It was pretty much normal to me. Then one day, my boss looked at me, frustrated, and said, "Sarah, you are not normal."

Growing up, I was taught to be a good girl, go to college, get good grades, meet a nice guy, get married, have some kids, get a respectable job, bring home half the income. And I did it!

Who wouldn't be grateful for a predictable life where you and your partner have cushy jobs that pay the bills? Who wouldn't want to go to work, play nice with your coworkers, and have a boss who loves you? Thing was, in real life, it wasn't like that at all.

The "cushy" salary was just enough to pay the mortgage. Don't even think about getting the much-needed house repairs (which only sent me into debt, little by little).

Co-workers would often engage in petty office politics that made me feel like I was back on the schoolground, and the boss was usually horrible. I wondered for years why I didn't feel like I fit in. Why couldn't I just be grateful for what I had?

But instead of grateful, I felt suffocated. Like I was being forced away from the things I truly wanted to spend time on: my family, my creativity, helping others, and enjoying life. And it was oh so restricting.

While I had many things to be grateful for, I wasn't in control of my life. I was being controlled by life. Like the one evening per week I was required to stay late at work to accommodate patients who had day jobs and could only make it into the center in the evenings,

Although my boss required everyone in the department to do the same thing, saying, "After all, fair is fair," it frustrated me. Nobody cared that I was a single mom with a young son.

I wanted to be in control of my life. I wanted to call the shots. And I didn't want to be lectured that "fair was fair." I loathed the idea of spending time at work, when I wanted to be at home. Again, hard to say since I should have been grateful. I could hear my father's voice saying, "Imagine, Sarah, there are people who don't have jobs, at all! Just be happy!"

I couldn't help thinking—again and again—that my job just didn't fit my lifestyle. I wanted to be home with my son. I didn't want to be working at the hospital until 9:00 at night, just because my boss said I had to.

Not only did I feel constricted by the confines of the rat race, it also didn't provide the security my father had dreamed of for me.

Because I was in the research world, the funding for my job was dependent on writing grants—and I did *a lot* of grant writing. Even though on paper my job was a permanent position at the hospital, my boss would frequently remind me of the reality: "Well, Sarah, you better make that grant good because if we don't get that funding, I don't know if you're going to have a job." That was her bizarre way of motivating me, but rather than inspire me, it made me feel incredibly insecure, as if I had zero job security. If the hospital ran out of funding, I would be cut from the position, and I always feared I'd be first to go.

It felt deflating that I had gone to school for six years and got a master's degree, and I was stuck in an environment where my job could be cut at any time. Where was the security that a traditional job was supposed to provide?

But it wasn't just that; I didn't fit in. I wasn't able to let things slide off my back. I was too sensitive. After a particularly hard meeting where I didn't see eye-to-eye with my boss about how the research was being done, she looked at me with a frustrated expression and said, "Sarah, you're not normal."

I couldn't even respond because the tears immediately began welling up in my eyes. I walked out of her office, holding back the tears until I got to my desk. While I knew deep down that maybe it was true, it really hurt to hear it said out loud and in such a cruel way. I started asking myself all kinds of questions. *Did I need to hear it? Even if it was true—did she need to be so ... mean? So harsh?* It was one of the toughest moments of my career.

As I walked down the hallway, each step I took filled me with more resolute certainty than I had ever had before that I would find a way out of this situation. At that time, I didn't know how. But I pulled up my big girl pants and asked myself what I could learn from the situation so I could at least keep the paycheck coming while I sorted out what the heck I was going to do.

In retrospect, years later, I can freely admit: my boss was right! There is nothing "normal" about me. Okay, debatably no one is "normal," but I've since learned entrepreneurs are a little bit different by nature. We are willing to take risks where others cower. We are willing to work 60 hours a week for ourselves (happily!) rather than 40 hours a week for a boss who calls the shots.

We are OK with looking like insane people who go after the lives of our dreams. We are OK with failing, so long as it means we went out trying. Why? Because it's on our own accord. We call the shots. And our potential? Unlimited. And that unlimited potential is like the carrot on the end of the stick for the donkey. It keeps us going.

Even though that moment was in 2016, my business search had actually started years prior, one night in 2010. I was on YouTube, late at night (you know what a rabbit hole that can be.) and came across Marie Forleo's channel, back in her early days.[1] Suddenly the light bulb went off for me. I thought, *A business is the golden key to the life I really want.*

This thought was completely averse to what I had been taught—you know, go to college and get a good job so you don't have to be a miserable entrepreneur!

Having grown up in a family of entrepreneurs, I was completely aware of just how much work was involved with running your own business—how much tenacity, commitment, vision and staying power was needed to stay the course. And truthfully, I had seen the stressful and sad parts of unsuccessful businesses, too. All of this, I'm sure, is why my dad wanted so badly for me to go to college; he thought I

[1] https://www.marieforleo.com/

would have it easier than he did. After years of avoiding the life of an entrepreneur, I was now seriously considering it—seeing the advantages it might offer me.

But I had a young child to support, so I continued to put on my game face at work. Behind the scenes though, I was working like mad to make my business dreams come to fruition. Even at work I was online constantly, trying to figure out business ideas while I was supposed to be doing some mundane task.

That sounds horrible, and I hate to say it: I was there out of necessity. I know with 100% certainty that I wasn't meant to work in an office, at least not forever. I felt like an alien at work! I felt like the only one who wasn't happy with a 2% annual raise, two weeks of vacation, and paying enormous daycare bills during the summer just so I could get to work. I thought it was bizarre that I was supposed to spend more time with the people at work than with my own son. I knew I had something to offer outside of the confines of the 9-to-5 life. Something creative, an idea that other people may have not thought about. And the more I learned, the more I realized that it may not be so hard to start making a respectable income online, all while helping others, being creative, and spending more time at home.

Maybe it could even be easy, right? Well, ha. Let's have a laugh about that!

But the reality is what could (and maybe even should) have been a straightforward path in business turned into an extremely long and windy road to success.

When I started my business, I dreamed of quitting my day job within a year. I ended up staying at my 9-to-5 job until 2018. If you have ever read Tim Ferris's book, *The 4-Hour Workweek*, or have listened to his podcast, you will know that he loves reading the case studies of folks who have made it work.

He emphasized this point in one of his podcasts:[2] "… these people who succeed very rarely throw caution to the wind and just quit their jobs without income in place. They typically do it after moonlighting and working evenings or weekends to prove that their new business works. In some cases, they will wait the span of one or two or three years, even if they get the flywheel spinning, just to double and triple confirm."

See, what should have taken me a year, ended up taking me seven long years to find the right path.

And I have since learned that certain businesses (ones in high demand) can even take a shorter time to get going. Since 2011, I've started a lot of different businesses, and over time, I have identified the ingredients that make a business work. Really work. I've seen again and again the places that are easy—far too easy—to get stuck.

I wrote this book because I saw too many women wasting their precious time, energy, and health on launching businesses that were not going to give them the freedom, time and money that they desired.

One of my biggest gripes is that women are so over-targeted with hundreds of crappy business ideas, and I know because I was caught in too many of them! There are hundreds of multi-level marketing schemes (MLMs), virtual assistant gigs, coaching, copywriting, and affiliate businesses out there. The list truly goes on and on.

While I respect and understand the great community that can be found in MLMs, the reality is that you most likely won't find freedom

---

2 https://tim.blog/2018/06/07/one-person-businesses-that-make-1m-per-year/

there. How many women in North America have devoted at least $50, $100, or $1,000 to an MLM that didn't get her any further ahead?

I was introduced to the MLM world at 18 years old when my "friend" from work suggested a nice dinner. Sure, why not?! I was flattered I had met such a nice friend and seemingly out of nowhere we really got along well.

When she opened up her briefcase full of Amway, my first thought was, "I wonder how quickly I can get out of here?" I was disappointed that my "friend" probably wasn't a friend at all. But the only way I could get her out the door was to sign up for the $30 starter package (which I thought I'd cancel later—I did after forgetting about it for several months!)

Throughout the years, I bought into a couple other MLMs with the small hope that I'd be the one-in-a-million to strike it rich. I know I'm not the only one who has experienced this feeling of hope. It's kind of like buying a lottery ticket and just hoping that *This Ticket Will Be the One.*

It's not just MLMs. As women, we're targeted with a lot of equally difficult business ideas that put us into prisons of expectation and false hope. In many cases, you fear it's probably not even going to work (like the MLMs). If you pick one that could potentially work, like maybe social media management or virtual assisting, you are stuck at an hourly rate of pay. These types of businesses are unfortunately a glorified work-from-home prison because women are kept so busy delivering their services, they don't have time to find new clients.

I intend that this book will be both practical and inspirational. I'll start by sharing about my journey as a business owner and how I finally—by trial and error—waded through the overwhelming labyrinth of online businesses to find the *right* business and created the seven-figure success I have achieved today.

I will start by sharing some of my stories in hopes that it will help you become clear on what you want (you will likely see yourself in some of my stories.) I believe we need more female entrepreneurs talking about what it was *really* like to get started—the good parts and the bad.

Then we'll talk about the crucial mental shifts you need to "make it" in the way you think to become a successful business owner. These chapters will help you to cultivate the true tenacity and conviction you need to succeed as an entrepreneur. Concepts we are not taught in school (but should be)!

Finally, we'll get practical (and fun!) and talk about the most important business concepts you need to consider before starting a business, so you don't start the wrong business, like I did. And if you already own (or owned) a business, these chapters will be instrumental in helping you make the adjustments needed to realize the business of your dreams.

In this book, you will discover how to start a work-from-home business quickly and simply. I'll give you the tools to identify a worthwhile business in a no-fluff way. And best of all, you'll learn how to make serious money online.

Also, I want to point out the obvious: I'm not a celebrity. My media features have been thin. With one of my businesses, I was on national TV in Canada a few times. Only recently have I been featured in *Entrepreneur* magazine.

With my digital advertising business (which I'll discuss later in the book), I've made a lot of money without having any media features and no real audience. It's my clients who have been featured on Oprah, "Good Morning America," and in *Forbes*. Instead, I've been that quiet, behind-the-scenes driving force on multiple million-dollar launches for my clients and in the process made an extremely respectable $50K per month revenue as an ads manager.

That's the wonderful thing: to be truly successful, you don't need to have all "the stuff." No TV. No brochures. No box of samples. You don't even need to have a fancy website to get clients to pay you really, really well.

This book is for you if you want to take control of your life and really do the things that matter to you and not live by the rules that society tells us. I will help you cut through the fluff.

Let's be practical and proactive and realize that there are some businesses where it's kind of like you're digging for gold and hoping to strike it rich. But some businesses, if you're really careful about your research, are the equivalent of selling shovels during the gold rush. I want to teach you to sell the shovels during the gold rush.

The online business space is projected to grow by about $15 billion in the next five years. So why don't we recognize what actually makes for a skill that you can learn and do quickly? That's what I'm going to help you do in this book.

Yes, I grew up—like so many—with the "go to college/get a job/get married/have kids" mantra all around me. I'm not saying that the rules and expectations in our culture are bad; I've got kids myself and life wouldn't be the same without them. What I *am* saying is "Why be normal?" I have learned through trial and error that you can actually make way more money, doing something that affords you more freedom and control over your life, and be your unNormal, awesome self! And I will teach you how to do it.

CHAPTER 2

A FAMILY OF ENTREPRENEURS ... AND THEN THERE WAS ME

"Sarah, go to school. You've got the privilege of getting an education."

My father wanted a better life for me than the one he had, and like most people of his generation, he believed a college education was the ticket to success. So, I listened to my father (the good girl I was!) and became the first person in my family to earn a college degree.

My family of entrepreneurs discouraged me from following in their footsteps because of the stress, uncertainty, and unpredictability of entrepreneurship. My father owned several businesses throughout his life. He sold cars and owned several gas stations and car repair shops.

To be honest, my dad would never have been able to work for someone else. He had this idea that if you had the opportunity to do something more, then you should. His view was that those people with higher education, like doctors and lawyers, were somehow better than he was although he may not have admitted this, and he wanted me to be entitled to that respect, too. He encouraged me to reach my full potential and avoid the second-rate life of a struggling entrepreneur by getting an education and a predictable job. It was a generational belief. You've probably heard this from your parents and grandparents: "Get an education!"

And while my dad always pushed me toward academics, he didn't realize he was modeling sales skills that I would come to recognize and appreciate later in life. He taught me a lot about sales without me knowing it, and he really taught me a lot about the entrepreneurial mindset.

In sales, you hear a lot about "the ask." My dad would often say things to me like, "What's the worst they can say? No?" He also taught me how to negotiate. Never mention a number first; always say, "Well, what do you want to pay?" Because, he said, "as soon as you put a number out there, bam! It's settled." That's the kind of thing he taught me for fun.

Once, when I was about 12 years old, my dad took me out for ice cream. When the guy behind the counter handed me my cone, I looked down at it and I complained to my dad, "Hmmm. That's kinda small."

My dad took my cone and handed it back to the guy, "Hey, we want to add a little more to that scoop. My daughter's not happy." And the guy said, "No." Can you believe it? Just, "No," without any explanation.

We walked away, with my dripping, puny ice cream cone, and my dad said, "You know what? That guy shouldn't own a business. He doesn't even know what customer service is."

It reminds me of that expression "penny wise and pound foolish." My dad demonstrated to me that the guy would have lost two pennies if he had to put a small bit more ice cream on my cone, but then he would have gained happy, returning customers. He lost future sales for a few cents.

There are many little things like that, which my dad shared with me about the entrepreneurial mindset.

My grandparents owned many businesses, too, including a photocopy shop, a beauty salon, and many real estate investments.

My grandma came over on a boat from Scotland in the 1940s. Back in the 80s, my grandma went to a real estate seminar after which she went on a buying blitz and snapped up 10 houses. For all of Grandma's business mishaps, this was an extremely good decision, because those investments sustained her financially for the rest of her life and through many other business disasters.

The people in my family didn't run their businesses out of choice, but out of necessity. We came from a lower to middle-class background. My parents did not have an education beyond high school. My parents and grandparents said they were in business because they lacked the college degrees they felt they needed to get an office job. Now I realize those choices were more genetics than they probably realized, and I'd bet money they all would have hated working in an office!

My dad was a workaholic—an excellent father, but he worked incessantly. I credit him with my strong work ethic and refusal to give up. He was an exceptional salesperson and worked most of his career selling used cars, which as you probably know, is one of the toughest types of sales because of the negative stereotypes associated with used car salesmen.

But my dad was classy and extremely good at speaking and relating to people. He needed to sell three cars a month just so he could pay the rent and utilities, and he always did. While my brothers and I were always provided for, it came at a great cost, and we could see it clear as day on our parents' faces.

My parents went through a phase when they were really successful at business. They bought a house in one of the best neighborhoods of our city. But then shortly after, my parents got divorced and by the time they split up the assets, they lost most of the money they had made during the "good" phase.

I saw the rollercoaster ride of entrepreneurship. And even during periods of success, my dad was an extreme worrier and was always thinking about business, even in his off-hours.

I'd also seen him go through the crummier parts of business, like firing the store manager who stole from him for over a year, or the business partner who caused him to lose his car dealership (which caused him to go bankrupt).

Business seemed scary and unpredictable to me. Witnessing my family's struggle and uncertainty gave me a negative attitude toward entrepreneurship.

So I understood why Dad pushed me in a more secure direction; I'm sure having had his experience, I would have been tempted to do the same.

I believed what my dad always said: that I was incredibly lucky to live a life so privileged that I could go to college. My dad really pushed education because he didn't want me to be stuck in the entrepreneurial trap. "This is going to be so good for you," he said.

Being the obedient daughter, I became the first person in my family to graduate from college and received my bachelor's degree in 2004 and a Master's degree in Anthropology 2006. And, YUP! It really is as useless a degree as it sounds. OK, I am kidding a bit, but seriously, not the best degree to get for employability.

Watching my family struggle, and fulfilling my father's wish, are the reasons why I never considered entrepreneurship. It turns out though, that it's really hard to change your DNA, because years later, there I was with the education and the job and the mortgage when I realized that this path wasn't actually making me happy. I was stuck in the rut of the 9-to-5 life.

How I knew I didn't fit in: The call of the entrepreneur

It took me years to realize I didn't fit into a standard life. But if I had known some key things, I would have recognized a lot earlier that I would never fit in, and there was no point trying.

I was a square peg being shoved into a round hole. If you're reading this now, you may also know exactly how I felt. The hard part was I didn't have anyone to tell me any differently. I was doing what I thought was right and what was expected.

Let's talk about some of the clues that I should have known meant I really wasn't cut out for that standard 9-to-5 life.

50 first jobs

I was good at *getting* jobs. By the time I graduated university, I had landed and quit at least 50 jobs (nope, not kidding). My first job was at a coffee shop when I was a teenager. I worked there for two years, the longest I ever lasted at a job like that. Then I got a job at a shoe store. I worked one shift, and never went back. Got a job at a restaurant called Kelsey's. Did two weeks, then quit because the senior servers would get the best tables. I didn't want to grind away for two years before I made mediocre tips, so I quit that. I got a job at a flower shop, then 10 more restaurants. At one local diner, I quit after the first shift. I bounced around from one menial role to the next. I felt bad for disappointing the people at these workplaces, but I felt a deep anxiety that I couldn't make sense of at the time. I kept repeating the cycle over and over.

It became the running joke in my family, "Where are you working *today*, Sarah?" My mom is the most supportive mom in the world, but I'm sure that there were times when she thought I was a little crazy. Not only would I quit these jobs, but I would pull into the parking lot, sit in the car and cry before I had to go in. I felt powerless because I didn't know there were any other options available to me.

There were very few jobs that I applied for and *didn't* get. That should have been a clue right there. I was good at selling myself! I never applied for sales jobs, though—it just never crossed my mind, because I was shy and introverted.

At the root of it all, I wasn't driven by the idea of working like a dog to make other people wealthy. I was a hard worker, but I wanted to work hard for *myself*, something I realized in later years. I was (and am!) really driven by my own vision. I lacked the employee mentality that my coworkers had. They actually *seemed* to care about the action items on the agenda at our weekly meetings; whereas I was pretending to take meeting notes when I was really journaling about *why* I hated my life! Can you relate? How many times have you thought, *I don't mind working hard, I just want to work hard for myself!*

In my university years where I was hopping from one job to the next, I finally decided to stop searching for jobs I hated and applied for more student loan money so I could focus on school. I reasoned it was okay to go far into debt because I'd pay it all back when I got a great job after graduation (Hah! Those loans followed me around for 15 years—a fact they don't really broadcast when you're applying for student loans).

If I'm being honest, the reason I stayed in school so long was because I didn't want to join the monotony of *adult life*. Adult life is something that everyone surely has to succumb to at one point, right? A life where you work all week, come home, cook supper, collapse in bed, only to wake up the next morning and repeat.

Like many women in the same position, once I entered the working world, weekends were stressful, household catch-up days, and if I was lucky, I'd get a little time off on Sunday, which rarely happened. It was dreadful. It was tedious. Why couldn't I have the life I really wanted? The hard part was I didn't even know where to start. The creative, joy-filled lives in the movies (say for example the Kate Hudson roles where she is a book editor or advertising executive, in a high-powered New York City apartment) seemed totally out of reach.

Armed with my new master's degree, I went to a job placement agency. Surely they would put me on a successful career path, right? They sent me to a data entry agency. It was horrible. I walked into a huge room and everyone was at their desk typing, entering information from little slips of paper. It looked exactly how I imagined that expression, "A trained monkey could do it." Poor monkey. I spent the two most boring days of my life there and I didn't go back.

The lady from the placement agency called me the next day. She was crying. Really and truly crying on the phone. "Why would you do that? We got you this job and you just didn't go back?" I felt terrible. I didn't think I was a bad person, but obviously this was a bad thing I did. I apologized, "I'm so sorry (and I truly was); I can't explain why I did it." I felt bad. Really bad. But feeling bad wasn't enough to get me back to that office that day.

Let me be really clear for a moment: I never felt like I was above the people at any of these jobs. What I did feel was a lot of shame because I thought there was something wrong with *me*. Part of it was just dread, not dealing with that, and judging myself. I know now that after trying many jobs and being miserable at all of them, it is because, at heart, I'm an entrepreneur and I need to work for myself. But it felt incredibly lonely since I had no one to tell me that!

Since becoming an entrepreneur, I have met so many people who have shared similar stories. Of just not fitting in, of nearly being fired, of not being able to work for other people. Maybe you may have been through similar experiences and are feeling lost because of them.

What moments have you had in your life that may be clues that you might enjoy entrepreneurship?

Hitting the road: The search for my calling

After grad school and the data-entry job placement debacle, I was still trying to avoid "real" adult life. I convinced my husband at the time, Noam, to move out to the west coast with me. We packed up the van (a used vehicle from my dad's car lot, which he generously gave us) with all our stuff and our dog, Joe. We waved a teary goodbye to my dad and our life in Ontario and made the five-day drive across Canada to Vancouver.

I felt like I was finally following my dreams. Mine was to be a writer. We agreed it would be great to live in the mountains and be creative and enjoy life. I thought maybe we could just escape to the country and life would be that easy. Ha!

Plus, I had dreamed of being a writer since I was a child. At 16, I told my dad that I wanted to be a writer and that I planned to write a book about my parents' divorces. He looked at me and said "Sarah, can you imagine how many people have already written books about their parents' divorce? You should really do something more practical, like be a teacher!" My heart was crushed but I thought maybe he was right. I knew he loved me and was trying to push me in the right direction. Being that dutiful daughter I was, I set my dreams of being a writer aside.

But through meeting Noam, and his mother, my dream was reawakened. She encouraged me, "You'd be a great writer if you work at it!" When I told her partner, Mary, what my father had said when I was 16, she told me, "Do you know how many books have been written about Shakespeare? And it doesn't stop people from writing about Shakespeare every single year." She had a great point…and it made me feel alive with the potential.

Their belief in me gave me the permission I needed to try being a writer, and Noam was very supportive, too. Looking back, it's ridiculous to think that I would just sit down at the keyboard and suddenly, I would be a writer.

At 25 years old I didn't have much to say about life, but I was driven. I called all the local newspapers and asked, "What can I do? Can I write articles?" To my surprise, the editors actually said, "Yes." But I quickly learned they don't pay you. "If you want to write an article as a hobby, go for it," the editors added.

To get my foot in the door and show them what I could do, I attended a local play at the local outdoor theatre (I think it was called *the Stratford*) and wrote several reviews, which were published! I really tried hard to make it work. But as you may already know, writers can work at their trade for 10, 20, 30 years, maybe a lifetime, and never make a dime.

It only took me a few months in British Columbia before I realized that being a writer was a pitiful way to make money. Even though I had been published in a few local newspapers, it was all pro bono, so it really was more like a hobby.

I begrudgingly started applying for jobs and quickly found something that looked like my dream job at the local planning council of North Okanagan, in interior British Columbia.

Sure enough, I got hired as a lead researcher on a homelessness project. *Woo-hoo!* I thought. Here was my opportunity to put my undergraduate degree in anthropology to work. My life was *finally* coming together.

Most people think of Indiana Jones when you say "anthropology," but that is just one subfield. It is really the study of humans, culture, and belief systems. Some anthropologists move to other countries and live there for many years, studying the culture and the people, then write books about them. I remember reading a riveting book about an anthropologist who moved to Afghanistan and lived with a terrorist group. He wanted to unravel how the terrorists thought, listen to the narratives that they were telling themselves, and develop an understanding of why they fought, in an effort to help.

This research job gave me the opportunity to do fieldwork without moving to a dangerous country. After all, I also wanted to start a family.

"Doing fieldwork" in this case, meant "on the streets," interviewing homeless people. I would write up the interviews, then submit a report to the government on the needs of homeless people in the region. I loved the team I worked with. For a second, I felt like I fit in. I didn't mind going to work and I enjoyed the 45-minute drive through the mountains to town each day and back.

It was a wonderful project, and I was really passionate about it. It paid $25 an hour, which at that time, I thought was pretty good money, being fresh out of school. But the job didn't last; it was a government-funded project that only had a life of six months.

At the end of the project, there I was again, with a graduate degree and nothing to really show for it.

Everywhere I followed my passion, I hit a wall against actually getting paid well for it

So there I was, searching for another job. I quickly found one at a local job placement agency and that's when the dread of "real" life set in. I was sitting in a tiny office all day, with barely anything to do. I had a very frustrating co-worker who was not my boss, but pretended to be. She would bother me when I didn't do anything and truly, there was nothing to do but she wanted me to be pushing papers and dusting the books all day just to look busy.

THIS was the life I had been dreading. I had come to the conclusion that every job I truly liked and felt passionate about didn't pay well. I wanted to be a social worker. Paid terribly. I wanted to be a writer—paid even worse. I thought I could help by teaching—nope. Terrible pay too. And all the fancy jobs in the movies—like book editors—paid terribly too.

My degree in anthropology is one of the most useless degrees you can get, unless you want to be traipsing around North America looking for teaching positions that are few and far between (even then, they pay terribly.) There were so many things I thought I could do that would be fulfilling but they were essentially all helping positions that wouldn't pay very well.

I was lost.

I was standing in the kitchen one day in early summer when my dad called with the news that would forever change my life. He said, "Sarah, I've got stage four cancer. I don't know how long I have to live. Would you want to come home and help me?" I froze like a deer in the headlights. I don't remember what I said but I remember feeling like I was stung by a swarm of bees. I stammered out some words of encouragement, but I knew stage four was bad.

I decided to get on a plane and get home immediately. Things were not going well in British Columbia, anyway. I was stuck in yet another job I hated, and Noam disliked the mountains, so we packed up and went home. I left immediately while Noam packed up the house and came home a few weeks later.

That time I nearly got fired

Back at home, Dad was ill, but not ill enough that I couldn't look for a job. My friend Natalie from university told me that the local research institute was looking for people, and that my degrees were enough to prove I knew the methodology to do research, even if I didn't have a medical degree.

I applied and got the job, which was another $25-an-hour government-funded research project. The job went well in the beginning, but I often felt like I was going through the motions. There were people there who took their jobs VERY seriously, and I felt like an imposter. I was only there to pay the bills, whereas the other people there wore business attire, had cards printed, and hobnobbed with the boss regularly at the company potlucks.

I had been assigned to head up a research grant submission. My coworkers were surprised to hear that our boss had assigned me to the job and seemed really concerned about my ability because it was a big project.

And they were right. I was in over my head. A Canadian Institutes of Health Research (CIHR) grant is one of the biggest grants you can apply for. Awards range from the hundreds of thousands to millions of dollars. I was completely unprepared even though I was hired to do those kinds of things; after all, I had written many research papers in university—how bad could it be?

Really bad. The week before the grant was due, I spent many sleepless nights trying to pull everything together, and my boss, who was livid about the whole thing, had to call in multiple favors from her colleagues to help my hobbling grant submission along.

We finally submitted the grant and then I collapsed. The stress had been unbearable, and I felt terrible that I had dragged my boss into the process with me. She had trusted me, and I let her down. We didn't get the grant. The chances of receiving it were slim anyway, but I still felt bad. The next week she came into the office and told me how extremely disappointed she was in me. And although I knew I deserved it, it was still hard to hear. Yet, she didn't fire me, and I couldn't figure out why. Maybe it was because at that time, I was pregnant and was due to start maternity leave in about a month.

After my son was born, I discovered why she hadn't fired me. I returned to the office after maternity leave and met with my boss to discuss the position that I assumed was waiting for me. She told me they had found someone who was a better fit for my job, but they would offer me a part-time position as an office assistant. OUCH!

Next to the time more recently, in 2017, that my newer boss told me I was "not normal," this was another instance of some of the deepest shame I have ever felt in my life. I remember the way she was looking at me, over the office table with the glare of the HR people by her side, hoping that I wouldn't call the labour board and complain that she had given my job away to someone else. The truth was, I knew I had blown it, and this was the natural consequence of cause and effect.

I took the office assistant position, and to add insult to injury, I had to share an office adjacent to the new person who had taken my job, Priyanga. My department had just submitted a new grant and Priyanga led it. She had done an exceptional job. Which I only knew because my boss went into her office and shut the door, but the walls weren't very soundproof, and I could hear everything that was being said. My boss spoke to Priyanga for 15 minutes about what a great job she had done and how impressed she was and how she would always give Priyanga a reference if needed.

I could have died right there.

If I ever needed proof that I indeed was a terrible office worker, that was it! My mind started racing about what else I could do. Do I just get another job? Do I try something different? Over the next several years that I remained there, I was constantly thinking of business ideas I could do. I took a copywriting course; and got a reiki certification to start. I was now only working part time since that's all they offered me, and that left me with a couple of days a week I could work on a business.

Have you ever been nearly fired?

Years later, now that I'm a full-fledged entrepreneur, I have since met many other entrepreneurs who have been fired. In fact, several were fired multiple times before they realized they had to do their own thing. The most common theme among entrepreneurs is a strong sense of independence. They question the status quo. They ask, "Is this all there is?" Many entrepreneurs are also very creative.

I have since realized that other entrepreneurs are often like me. They too often don't fit in. They hate petty office politics and feeling like they have to fake it to pay the bills. They too dreamed of something more before they even knew what that was.

This is where I invite you to listen deeply. If you hear that little voice that says, *I want something more*, that voice will not go away. It is our life's work to follow that voice. Even if your attempts don't work out, you can still say you tried. It is better to have tried and failed than to not try at all.

Only thing is, we are not equipped with the tools to think like entrepreneurs in a world that is tailored for 9–to-5 worker bees. In the upcoming chapters, I am going to help you prime your mindset to think more like an entrepreneur, so you have more inner resources to take action on your plans and build the beautiful life you dream of. Let's get started, shall we?

CHAPTER 3

LIFE MAKES PLANS FOR YOU

He's a great guy, but the wrong guy

I was failing at my career, and my personal life took a turn for the worse.

My father only lived for a year after we returned home and I went through the devastating experience of losing him. It was heartbreaking that he didn't live long enough to see the birth of our beautiful son, Blue.

Then, when Blue was three weeks old, Noam told me he was leaving me. I was in shock, but I didn't fight it. I accepted it. I was a brand-new mother, still on maternity leave, nursing every hour, trying to figure out how to get some sleep and when I could squeeze in a shower. While I couldn't visualize a future without Noam's support—emotionally or financially—I was too stubborn to beg him to stay. I now know it was my intuition kicking in for good reason.

When the shock wore off, I saw clearly and calmly that this was not the right relationship from day one; having a child served to illuminate that. Noam is a good person, but we just had different priorities. He wanted to do things his way and I wanted to do them mine. Separating was the right decision.

When people hear about the timing of when we broke up, they tend to jump to the conclusion that Noam is a monster, cruel for leaving me. That couldn't be further from the truth. He was kind and considerate of Blue and me. From the day we started trying to have a child we agreed that I would be a stay-at-home mom until Blue started school. Noam went above and beyond to honor that agreement by paying double the amount of court ordered child support. This was a hardship for him because he didn't earn very much at the time, but he provided enough income that I only had to work part time for a few years.

When Noam moved out, I suddenly had to take radical responsibility for my life because I realized I was on my own. That cozy feeling of security from a spouse had vanished. And that put me into fight-or-flight mode.

Still working at the hospital research department part-time (and desperate to quit), I was tooling around YouTube one night when I came across Marie Forleo's business coaching videos. I watched one, and then another, and another. She had set off a light bulb in my head: *Holy Toledo! I can start a business. This is what I need to do.*

I put my disdain and distrust of entrepreneurship to the side and I began the years' long journey of business ownership, starting with the raw food business.

When my father was diagnosed with cancer, I was in a frenzy to find a cure or at least something to slow down its progress. I also freaked out, thinking if cancer got him, it could get me, too. I bought my dad all sorts of concoctions, natural remedies, recipes, books, movies—the works—to try and stop the cancer in its tracks.

In my search, I happened upon a documentary by Kris Carr called, *My Crazy, Sexy Life*, which detailed her journey with cancer and how she used a plant-based diet to help transform her back to wellness. I got really serious about cleaning up my health and fell in love with a vegan, raw food diet. It's a diet used to not only nourish, but also to heal, and consists of mostly uncooked salads and vegetables (you would be surprised at how many dishes you can make with raw vegetables)!

While it was too late to make a difference for my father, I adopted a fully plant-based raw-food diet myself. Although there is a genetic component to cancer, my father's cancer type—colon cancer—is heavily linked to diet. I was scared silly that I'd get the same cancer he did if I didn't clean up my eating habits.

People started to take notice of my new healthy lifestyle and asked questions. "How do you survive on raw?" "How do you grow your own wheatgrass?" Having those conversations got me to thinking: *You know what? This could be my golden ticket to a successful business. I'll be a raw food teacher. I'm super passionate about it. I love helping people. I love talking about health.*

How not to start a business...

I was all in and wanted to start right way. Recently divorced by that point, I sold the house and had about $20K in savings. I took that, went to California, and enrolled in the Living Light Culinary Institute where I earned my certification as a raw food chef in just a few weeks. After all, I was used to degrees and certifications and taking classes. I needed a certificate, right? Wrong!

Certificate in hand, I returned home expecting clients to be banging down the door for my service. Hahaha! That's far from what happened. But I pulled out all the stops. I even had a kitchen sink custom built that I could take to the local church where I did my raw food classes.

Then I started doing all the nitty gritty of marketing my business: writing for local newspapers, going on national TV, getting published on *mindbodygreen.com* and a few other places, too. I was trying to do absolutely everything on the list to make my business profitable. My end goal was to make enough money to quit my job, which amounted to roughly a few thousand dollars a month. That way, I could help people, spend more time at home with my son, and be a smashing business success, too.

The raw food business did achieve a level of success that I'm proud of. After five hard years of burning the candle at both ends, I had built a great community of people. I was working the business, holding monthly potlucks, and teaching raw food classes on the weekend. The classes were a ton of work: transporting cooking supplies, bowls, dishes (even the sink, for goodness' sake!) to the local church, and I was still working part-time at my day job. I was dying from overworking myself because the business model did not allow for me to make enough money based on the hours I was putting into it. I was working my job. I was doing the business. I was trying to be a good mom, and I really got burnt out.

It was time to take a hard look at my path—where I was and where I was headed. More importantly, I needed to concentrate on where I wanted to *be*. What do I do next? This was where the business rabbit hole really began. I was desperate to succeed and started clamoring for things to make it work (and spent a lot of money trying to save it).

I considered becoming a health coach. I was already teaching people about the nutritional aspect of healthy living, so this seemed like the next logical step. I was aware of the top health coaching institutes and their claims about financial freedom, multiple revenue streams and how one call can change your life, so I went for it. I invested another $8K to get certified as a health coach. (Yup! Another useless certificate!)

Turns out, the school offered very little support and it was really a flimsy certificate. Even with the marketing experience I had gained through the raw food business, health coaching didn't make a difference in my income either. Clients were still not paying me enough for my time.

The few clients I had were paying me about $120 an hour, which sounds alluring, but really, I had created a work-from-home prison. Even if I filled out all my hours in a day, I would still only make max $700-ish a week. When I booked all the hours in a day, there was no time left to search for new clients, so it was at least half of that $700 that I truly took home.

On to the next thing

I knew I was successful at packing my raw food classes with 50 and more people, so I thought, *Maybe I can teach people how to have a raw food business.* Within a few months, I put together a class on how to have a banging successful green smoothie business; basically, how to create a really successful raw food business for a respectable part-time income. I even won an award for this program from the coaching institute that certified me, but again, although my course on how to start a raw food business was quite popular, it didn't generate enough sales.

I was going further and further into debt—more than $30,000 at that point. I began to realize that my business wasn't a business; it was an expensive hobby. On the front end, it looked successful; I was being featured in publications, my living room was packed with people who wanted to learn how to do a raw food detox, yet I still wasn't able to pay the bills.

I would get Blue off to school, drive to the hospital, work, come home, make him supper, give him a bath, put him to bed … and then I would work from eight until midnight trying to market my business. I was exhausted every minute of the day.

In 2015, after years of trying to make a decent profit, I accepted it was not going to generate the income I was seeking, and made the decision to close every part of my raw food business (the demos, the coaching and the course).

The only option I felt I really had was to take my career more seriously.

I finally quit the part-time job I had been demoted to, and began the search for new opportunities. I was thrilled that within a matter of months, I had two job offers. I went with a research and coaching job at a local hospital. My years being a health coach combined with my research skills helped me score this job.

But the environment was tough. The people weren't that friendly, and it was highly competitive. My boss often said to us at team meetings that if anyone wanted to quit, it would be no skin off her back since there were hundreds of people vying to get our spaces. She worked hard to make us feel replaceable, so we'd scramble and work overtime.

Based on all that I learned from my epic failure with the first grant I ever wrote, the one that nearly got me fired at the previous job, I had developed the experience needed to be an expert grant planner. I used those skills in this new position and went on to submit many successful, expertly-executed grants.

I was still licking my wounds from my last business, though. I wasn't exactly sure what had gone wrong, but I knew one thing: You can have a really amazing business idea and deep passion for it, but if it doesn't meet a demand—a niche in the marketplace where people are willing to pay you for what your time is really worth—you're not going to get any further ahead. You're going to get stuck in a work-from-home prison, or the amount of money you're able to make will be severely limited.

It didn't seem like the right time to build another business as I was severely in debt. I tried to convince myself to be happy and to some degree I succeeded. Blue was resilient and didn't mind daycare and I got into the habit of living the 9-to-5 life. I told myself I was lucky to have the job.

Everyone who knew me knew that I had tried to get a business up and running and had failed at it. My new coworkers found videos of me blending smoothies on YouTube. One co-worker even broadcast this on a projector at work during a meeting with my senior supervisors and everyone started laughing. I felt like a huge failure. It was a really humiliating and heartbreaking time in my life. I felt completely defeated. In an effort to deflect pity, I used to joke that "I would rather work 40 hours for someone else than 80 hours a week for myself."

The bright side is I got my personal life back. I started dating again, something I had no time for while I was trying to run a business. I met my current partner, Joachim, and quickly got pregnant.

Then history started to repeat itself! I don't know if it was the pregnancy hormones or what, but suddenly I was thrust back into the same longing and desire for my own business.

My daughter Avigael was born in late 2016 and by 2017, I was having a sort-of business déjà vu. My partner's salary was not enough for me to be a stay-at-home mom, and once again I was faced with trying to figure out a way to make enough money to be at home with my children. I figured for all of my business failures, I should surely be able to make a business work now.

And you know, I was kinda right!

It had been a while since I'd tried my hand at a business, but I knew I had to. I asked my mom to watch my daughter during some daytime hours (my son was in school at that time) so I could work on the business, and she totally agreed. My mom is my biggest fan and always supported my business dreams. Thank you, Mom!

I was far savvier by that point and knew I needed a skill. I started out with copywriting, thinking this would bring in clients that pay well.

I quickly realized that was not the case. There are thousands of people putting their name up on job boards and hoping and praying that someone's going to choose their profile over all the others. The best strategy is to create an impressive Upwork profile and hope someone reaches out to you. Not really a strategy at all, if you ask me.

Problem was, I couldn't even create an Upwork profile: they denied me since my profile resembled too many other people's profiles on the platform! Regardless, it's a tedious process. You can spend a lot of time creating the profile and negotiating with potential clients without ever getting much work. Combine that with the fact that the people who go to those job boards to hire are looking for writers in specific niches, with the lowest rates.

One day, while listening to a podcast, I heard the guest say that Facebook ads were the missing piece to business success. If you can get Facebook ads to work for you, you can make a lot of money. Aha! I immediately felt that THIS was the missing piece! Facebook ads for my new business idea! (At that time, I was hovering between copywriter and consultant.)

The very next week, I hired someone who called herself an "Ads Manager," and I paid her $2,000 a month to run the ads for my business. After two months … nothing happened. Crickets. I think I got maybe one phone call from a potential client. Again, I had failed, and I thought: *How can this happen now? Me knowing so much and being savvy. How could I, yet again, fail at business?* I was checking off all the boxes. I was doing free consults. I was joining Facebook groups and striking up conversations with people and it just wasn't working.

The Ads Manager I hired said to me, "Just be patient; this can take some time. Sometimes it can take six months, even 12 months." Holy cow! I did not have that amount of time or money to invest. I couldn't help but notice that she was very successful with a staff of 10 and about 40 clients.

Oh, wait! I am in the wrong business

That afternoon, I reached out to the five Facebook contacts I had at the time, and asked, "Would you want my help with Facebook ads?" Three out of five of them replied with an immediate "Yes!"

Wow! I knew instantly I was really onto something (being an Ads Manager) because I had never had that kind of response before with any of my other businesses. I was always chasing people down the street to get them interested in what I was doing. That little initial positive feedback was all I needed. I immediately invested a tidy sum for someone to teach me the deeper knowledge I needed to run the ads.

Within six weeks I had my first client from Australia, who paid me $10,000 to do a three-month project. She wound up staying with me for six months. That first client paid for my initial investment. That was when I learned: *When you're in the right business, you accel-*

erate quickly. You are not in purgatory for five years waiting for the business to start when you've got a hot service.

I made my investment back in 90 days. The client paid me $6,000 for month one, and then $2,000 for each month thereafter and she signed a three-month contract (which is roughly $14K Canadian).

This was in January of 2018. In my first three months I got three clients and then I paused for a month because I wanted to catch up with the deliverables. Then I started running my ads again (because not only did I run ads for my clients as their Ads Manager, I also ran ads for myself to get advertising clients). By July, I had five clients. By September, I was up to nine clients. By October of that first year, I was up to 14 clients, which is roughly $25K per month. The business was accelerating really fast, and I needed to hire someone to help me (great problems to have, right?)

I worked and worked on this service and it showed. Being an Ads Manager was a simple and highly valued skill, so getting paid well wasn't that hard. And people kept saying "Yes!" to working with me.

Going back to the earlier days, in 2018, my goal was to quit my research job in three months. I found that when I was still working, I could only manage five clients at a time. The way this thing was snowballing, I had no doubt I could increase that number.

For 10 years I had fantasized about the moment I would quit my job. It played in my head like a scene from a movie. I would barge into that woman's office and dramatically announce, "I quit!"

April of 2018, just six months into my new ads business, the day had come. Rather than barging, I walked somewhat demurely into my boss's office (Yes, the same boss who had told me earlier that I was NOT normal), and told her that I had an announcement. I informed her that I was resigning from my position.

She looked up from her desk, and replied, "Really? Why? What are you doing?"

"Well, I've got a business now."

"Really? Doing what?"

"Ads Manager with Facebook ads."

She was completely perplexed. I might as well have been speaking a foreign language.

"What do you mean?" she asked.

I had to explain to her what they were. "You know how when you're on Facebook, you see ads? Well, I create them on behalf of other businesses who need to advertise." She was dumbfounded. She didn't even realize that this was a thing. (Many people still don't.)

The meeting took all of five minutes and ended with her saying, "Okay, good luck. Let me know if you need anything." No drama. No shock. No scene, like from that movie, *Jerry McGuire*, when he's fired from the agency, and he makes that big speech in front of all those people. I was expecting it to be like that, but obviously I'm a shy and introverted person, so that would never have happened. It was a very quiet end to a fantasy I had stoked for 10 years.

That moment may have been anticlimactic, but the truly exciting thing was after that day, my business climbed over the next two years to $57K *a month* in revenue (yes, you read that right. After two years I was making nearly as much per month as I was per year at the hospital job).

By leaving my job, I was able to focus on growing my agency, continually work on my craft, and learning new strategies. I started living the life of an entrepreneur. I was getting out there, meeting people, networking, and investing in mentorship. And I loved it!

I want everyone reading this to know I truly (finally) felt at home as an entrepreneur. I no longer felt like there was something wrong with me. I now know what my dad and mom and grandparents felt by wanting to be entrepreneurs, versus working for someone else. I now know what pushed every other entrepreneur out there to succeed. They have drive, they have hustle, and they have a vision to set their own rules and not work for someone else. If you have felt the same way I did, if you feel that way now, I promise you your tribe is out there. There are other people, budding entrepreneurs, who also don't fit in and have yet to find their place.

I'm not saying there's anything wrong with working for someone else's vision; I appreciate and admire people who apply themselves to someone else's vision and believe in it. We need that in the world. But for those who are called to be an entrepreneur, it's nearly impossible to do anything else. We need that in the world too.

If you're a woman raised like I was, you have probably considered a range of "helping" professions. But we can help people in a business as well (something that never crossed my mind when I was young).

All the "helping" jobs I considered while I was growing up paid terribly. Helping people has been a consistent theme throughout my entire life, and the raw food business had provided a wonderful opportunity to do that. I don't know if we're kind of bred that way as women to think about serving others, but that was truly a guiding force for my business.

I didn't just want to make money, I wanted to help people with my passion for living long, healthy lives. I just didn't know how to apply that feeling of wanting to help people in a way that would also allow me to live a life without being constantly burnt out from working long hours for little pay.

Entrepreneurship is ever-evolving, and you can have it on your own terms

By 2019, I had rapidly grown my ads agency successfully, and realized in order to get to the next level in my business, I needed to hire more staff.

But I was stuck because I didn't want a business with 20 people to manage. As an introvert, I want plenty of time to myself. My ideal week doesn't include managing people every minute of the day.

Again, I was feeling the itch of something more. It was time to diversify because I'm a multi-passionate entrepreneur with shiny object syndrome. It was time for some business mentorship, some guidance about how to channel my energy and talent.

I began working with a mentor in California who said to me, "Why don't you teach people how to do this? You've always wanted to help people, and now you've got a successful business, you could absolutely show other people how to do it."

My response was, "No way!" I doubted myself because I didn't know what I would teach, but he really encouraged me and helped me overcome a lot of self-doubt. Even though I'd been good with the agency, it's a completely different thing to teach those skills to others and I wasn't sure I had the confidence to pull it off.

Here's the truth: when you start something new, you likely won't have confidence. Confidence arises from doing something over and over; from mastering a skill. Most women get stuck because they think they need confidence to start a business. But really, they just need courage—the courage to draw a line in the sand and say, "I'm starting a business now."

I started without being fully convinced I knew it would work. But what did I have to lose? I overcame my self-doubt by focusing on helping people. Instead of overthinking it, I just got to work. I knew I had something I could teach people that would be really valuable to them. My business mentor continued to encourage me by reminding me that I could help people by sharing the path I took and the lessons I learned—from multiple-failed businesses to amazing success, based on an in-demand skillset.

It would have been a very easy and natural progression to go bigger and increase the size of the ads management agency by hiring more people, but I have remained true to my original motivation. I have always wanted a business that fit my lifestyle, and my lifestyle is focused on spending time with my children. I'm making a lot of money using a fairly simple skill, and I love teaching others how to do the same thing.

At heart, I'm a coach. Back in my hospital research days, I was coaching patients on how to reduce their risk of heart disease and writing grants to get the money to do that. In the raw food business, I was coaching people on how to eat healthier. I've always had a huge passion for teaching people. It therefore made more sense to not build the agency vertically, but to vary the model by keeping the agency where it was, and building it outward into a mentorship program. It was right in front of my face, but I didn't see it. That's where my mentor, Scott, came in. He saw it immediately. (This is the value of working with a mentor.)

Let's stop talking big figures and talk profit

It wasn't until 2018 that I learned what a profit margin was. Gulp. I mean, I'd heard the term, but it was really a jargony business word that confused me. (This is my other mission—to educate women on business concepts they may not know, like I did.) A profit margin is what you make from your business, meaning how much actually ends up in the bank after you pay your business expenses.

I didn't learn this until I called up my brother, Aaron, and told him I had hit 100K before the first anniversary of my business. In his no-nonsense style, he said, "I don't care if you hit 100K; that's just a number! What is your profit margin?" I took a moment to Google that and told him I'd have to get back to him with that answer. (Because I didn't know it.)

Good news! Twenty percent is generally considered to be a high profit margin.[3] My ads management agency profit margins were at roughly 50% - 60%! Meaning after I got paid, and paid my expenses (taxes, consultants, and any software fees) I roughly kept 50 to 60% of what I got paid.

A lot of people like to throw around flashy figures of, "Oh, I've made a million bucks." A more important business consideration is: what are your profit margins? If you're like my brother who owns a bunch of bakeries, he's happy with an 11% profit margin. Profit margins for brick-and-mortar businesses are much lower (obviously, as they have to rent physical space and employ many staff, they have more expenses to pay.) With an online ad business, you can say, "Hey, I make a lot of money, and have really great profit margins, too. A lot of it goes straight to my savings account."

Making extremely good money working from home, being creative, and helping other people may seem like a far-fetched dream. My business journey taught me that most people grow discouraged because they choose the wrong business model, not because it's impossible to succeed. It really is possible to create a successful business if you focus on the right skills. With the right attitude and drive, you can reach your dream, too. I'll talk a bit more about that in the coming chapters.

---

3 https://corporatefinanceinstitute.com/resources/knowledge/accounting/profit-margin/

CHAPTER 4

BECOME OBSESSED

Are you different too?

As anyone who knows me will attest to, I'm a bit different, like many entrepreneurs! As a teenager, I became so obsessed with one of my favourite sitcoms, *Full House*, that I literally used to write out the script for the shows. This was a pastime of mine as a kid.

Because the sitcom made me feel so good, I would record it on VHS, then I would get my pad of paper, pen, and the remote, and I would stop and start the show while I wrote down who said what. I was obsessed with the show and created a large collection of scripts. When I was done with transcribing enough episodes, I started transcribing scripts for other movies and shows I loved. Writing the scripts allowed me to live a little longer in that world. Plus, I loved the written word.

My obsessions weren't just reserved for writing scripts; whenever I love something I have thrown myself into it 100%. When I started eating raw, I was fanatical about it. I didn't want to ingest even one meal that wasn't healthy. I know this sounds kind of crazy but I'm going to talk about why it's important.

No matter what type of business you start, you have to be prepared to be single-mindedly obsessed with your goals. Growing a successful business takes more tenacity, courage, and repeatedly showing up (even in the face of failure) than most people could possibly realize. Even if you have a skill that's in demand like advertising, you are always hitting up against your own most self-limiting beliefs. Your capacity to make money is directly related to the level of personal evolution work you can do.

Your capacity to make money is directly related to your willingness to work on yourself, not just your business. This means taking time for personal reflection, being open to change, and developing new, healthier attitudes toward yourself and toward money.

If you're not willing to grow and evolve as an entrepreneur, you're going to severely cap the type of progress you're able to make as a business owner. To succeed in business, you have to be obsessed with your goals and obsessed with your vision.

I have yet to hear of a successful entrepreneur who wasn't obsessed with his or her vision. As Elizabeth Gilbert's best friend, Delia Shiraz, said in *Eat, Pray, Love*, "Having a baby is like getting a tattoo on your face. You kind of wanna be fully committed." There is a similar logic to owning a business. Sure, anyone can own a business, but many people aren't committed, and therefore are before not successful.

If you want to be successful at your business, you have to be as certain about wanting that business to succeed as you would be about wanting a tattoo on your face. This is precisely because there will be days that are hard, days that you want to give up—and without the unwavering obsession with your business and your goals, your chances of success will be much lower.

Obsession gets a bad rap

It drives me crazy when I hear people say, "Everything in moderation." I desperately disagree. For a small percentage of people, moderation works. But for far more people, moderation doesn't work at all. In fact, humans are notoriously bad at moderation.

For example, during my years coaching people to eat healthier, both in my own raw food business and with patients at risk of heart disease at the research hospital, the people who made gains in their goals were the ones who didn't practice moderation. They went headfirst into their goals. They tracked their food like crazy, they planned extensively, they tried new recipes, they bought gadgets to track their steps, and they joined Facebook groups of other people with similar goals.

Without a doubt, the people who make the commitment and become obsessed with their goals are the ones who reach them. Treating your business like its success is the only option will drastically increase the chances of it working out. I do not mean that you cannot stick to your day job until your business is up and running. I did this, and I recommend it so you can pay the bills.

You have to have the mindset of, "Failure is not an option." Plus, you need a deep-seated belief that you will succeed one way or another. Your simple belief that you are resourceful and will succeed is going to increase the chances of it happening. This is the hard part as it's kind of like putting the cart before the horse—but you need to do it!

We live in a culture that likes to make people who get obsessed with things feel bad about themselves. This is the aunt at your family gathering who derides you for being obsessed with your goal of writing a book. Or the friend who keeps pressuring you to eat a piece of chocolate cake saying, "Don't you ever have fun?"

What I've learned is that these people make us feel bad about our obsessions with our goals because those obsessions show strength and resilience that they don't have. It's often plain jealousy. (Also, they may not even be aware of what they are doing.)

If you want to have a successful business or great health, your odds of success are catapulted by your level of commitment.

The worst part about moderation is that one little thing can throw you off. First it's one cookie, then it's another cookie, then it's the whole bag. Before you know it, you've crossed a whole day of your diet off your list. Next, you've decided to start the diet on Monday.

In his famous book, *The 4-Hour Body*, Tim Ferris recommends you have a "cheat day." I cannot tell you how many people's cheat "day" turns into a cheat "weekend," and then it's not long before they give up altogether.

Willpower is a weak muscle

Willpower is a fair-weather friend. When we don't achieve our goals, we are often quick to beat ourselves up because willpower failed us. The truth is, many behavioral studies have shown that willpower is not something we can count on. In fact, if you rely on willpower to drive changes you want to make in your life, you most likely will not succeed.

What does drive success? Habit. This is true because there is no time, or indecision left to debate. When it comes to willpower, we literally have to will ourselves to do something. That means we need to internally debate, *Should I have the piece of cake, or should I just have the glass of water?*

In that period of debate, our defenses weaken. Soon enough, our brain has given us 10 good reasons why the cake is the right decision and then we have gobbled it up.

Now, if you look at things that are habits (for example brushing our teeth or making our bed in the morning) we waste zero time debating if we should brush our teeth. We just do it.

In business, in the absence of habit, we need obsession with our goals. You need to have the same level of certainty with your willingness to have a business. You have to go after your business as if it's the only path for you. You cannot waste any time or energy being indecisive.

So many times, I see women worry that chasing their business dreams is somehow irresponsible or selfish. I've felt that way many times as I was starting my business. In fact, even though my business was doing well, I was still plagued with feelings of guilt over quitting a job that other people would be dying to have.

But as podcaster Imogen Roy says, "If you were going to go on a road trip, would you put gas in the car?" We live in a puritan society that says we need to work first, *then* fuel ourselves, but if we are always running on empty, we won't have the energy (aka fuel) to live a fulfilled life. Women often put themselves last. I know this as I have been guilty of it myself. It takes a lot of effort to unwind this conditioning!

Owning a business can feel unbalanced at times. It is the tougher path than the standard 9-to-5, especially at first when you are trying to gain momentum—that's when it requires the most effort. Even with the dedication I feel for my family, and knowing they are my reason for everything, I am still obsessed with my business. There are days I spend with my family and all I can think about is business. Society would like to make us feel bad for this.

I remember watching a clip of motivational speaker Gary V answering a question from a nervous person in the audience. The audience member was feeling guilty for chasing his dreams. Gary V talked to him about the myth of balance and the futility of trying to live a life that is anything other than the life we really want to be living. If we are not trying to fulfill the calling that we hear deep inside, we will never be our true selves and we risk becoming bitter and resentful to the people around us.

Even now, as a successful business owner, I still work full-time at it. My business is something I'm passionate about. When my mom watched my daughter, I often felt guilty about pursuing my dreams. But working for my business, instead of a boring office job, made me feel alive. The potential was irresistible. Working hard for myself, and not someone else, gave me crazy drive to succeed and provide. As a woman, it brings out my masculine energy and success (and ultimately the freedom because of it) excites me in a way that words cannot describe.

This would have never happened if I didn't decide to stop apologizing for wanting to be a business owner. Society would love to guilt us into feeling like we aren't good parents unless we are sacrificing everything, and this simply isn't true.

Just the other day, a student of mine posted online that her family members had been visiting from out of town and her mother told her how disappointed she was that she was even thinking of working when she should be home with the children. The guilt she felt because of her mother's harsh comments was causing her to consider dropping her plans to start her own business as an ads manager, and walk away from the mentorship program. She was deeply discouraged because her family was judging her.

The responses from the other members of the group were overwhelming. In fact, 27 women spoke up to offer her encouragement. Members were supporting her (and each other), by reiterating that our families and our children will be just fine.

We all found this to be such a helpful exchange that I've included some of the responses here:

From Jennifer, "I am a recovering people-pleaser, especially with my parents. But I heard a quote that really resonated with me: 'People are going to judge, so you might as well do what makes you happy.' I still struggle with people-pleasing. But I've been more private with my journey and will just share only my wins with them since they also don't understand my choices, but ultimately, they are mine. And so are yours! I say go for it and trust your intuition."

Sarah added, "I am so sorry you are dealing with this. Your mother has two choices: She can offer to help you with your children if this is such a concern for her, or she can butt out. You know what's best for your situation and in the future if she can't respect that then let her know that you do not welcome these comments and you expect her to respect your decision. Time to set some clear boundaries. Again, I am so sorry. Our kids are going to be just fine."

Kelly said, "I can completely relate to you. Hang in there. We always want the approval and support of our parents, but sometimes ... it's not there. I like to file that away for my journey in raising my children in the 'things to not do' folder. I feel like in order to make the decision to invest in yourself in this mentorship program, your heart was telling you it was the path you needed to take to provide a certain type of life for your family. Trust your instincts! It'll be wonderful for the kids to be exposed to other people, caretakers, and experiences. It will be fulfilling for you to pursue a dream! You don't have to choose one or the other, and I think that's an amazing example to set for our kids, too. You're doing great."

Nadia contributed, "Gender roles are extremely limiting, and you DARE to be bolder than a label. Just remember she's just projecting her ideal reality, but it's not your world. Your feelings are valid. But living your reality is more important than hers."

And I said, "I remember a wonderful insurance lady I had a meeting with who said to me, the reality is her kids didn't really even remember who minded them as young children. She said, we, as parents, worry so much about this but at the end of the day they don't remember and honestly, they don't! Just the other day my son said something to me, and I said 'Blue, don't you remember all the times we went to the museum together? All the trips we took?' And he had to scratch his head and think twice about this."

What matters most is that we are happy parents, because happy parents are the best parents. Sure, there are other important ingredients but overall, I would wager a guess that the quality of time you spend with your kids is far more important than spending a whole bunch of time being miserable. In fact, research supports this. A recent study showed that spending a half an hour of uninterrupted time playing with your child was preferable to multiple hours while distracted.

In fact, it appears the sheer amount of time parents spend with their kids between the ages of three and eleven has virtually no relationship to how children turn out, has after and a minimal effect on adolescents, according to the first large-scale longitudinal study[4] of parent time to be published in April in the *Journal of Marriage and Family*. The finding includes children's academic achievement, behavior and emotional well-being."[5] For those more interested in learning about the research that supports this, I highly recommend the book, *Selfish Reasons to Have More Kids: Why Being a Great Parent is Less Work and More Fun Than You Think*, by statistician Bryan Caplan. (I know this

---

4 apps.washingtonpost.com/g/documents/national/does-the-amount-of-time-mothers-spend-with-children-or-adolescents-matter/1490/

5 https://www.washingtonpost.com/local/making-time-for-kids-study-says-quality-trumps-quantity/2015/03/28/10813192-d378-11e4-8fce-3941fc548f1c_story.html

paragraph will have some of you vehemently disagreeing, but I only ask you consider looking into the research as it's incredibly compelling.)

I am certainly not saying that you shouldn't spend time with your kids! Far from it—the main reason I started this whole business journey in the first place was because I wanted to be a hands-on parent. But I am calling out the societal belief (and the internal guilt) that we can't be obsessed with our passions and *also* be good parents.

It's OK to be obsessed with your goals, to go after the dreams you want. It's OK to try and fail. In fact, it's hard to run a successful business without some failures. It's far more courageous than not trying at all.

In fact, the sooner we get comfortable with disappointing other people, the sooner we can start living an unapologetic life that is truly of our creation. As Glennon Doyle says in *Untamed*, "Every time you're given a choice between disappointing someone else and disappointing yourself, your duty is to disappoint that someone else. Your job, throughout your entire life, is to disappoint as many people as it takes to avoid disappointing yourself." So, let's get practical. In order to get the right mindset about starting your business, you want to get in touch with why you're doing this, then adopt a "no-fluff" mindset. Let's dig in.

What are your goals?

In my mentorship program, the first thing I ask my new students to do is fill out a questionnaire that gets them to think about their goals.

In stating your goals and exploring what your ideal life looks like, you will have *that* much more clarity and—by extension—the appetite to stick to the path, even on the days you want to detour.

One of the first things I did when re-committing to my business journey in 2017 was to purchase *Think and Grow Rich* by Napoleon Hill. One of the first exercises in the book is about mapping out your exact "what" and "why." It's an extremely powerful way to stay the course.

Let's get started with …

What's your Why?

Why do you even want a business? What is it about the lifestyle that is speaking to you? There are as many answers as there are people asking the question. Your answer is as valuable as anyone else's. For many people it's going to be as simple as:

- I don't like my job.
- I want to spend more time at home with my family.
- I want to do something more meaningful and creative that helps people.
- I want to have more flexibility with my time to do what I want.
- I don't want a boss dictating how many hours of vacation I can take a year.

This is the first subject we tackle when I mentor women to become highly paid ads managers.

To discover your Why, grab a pen and paper, and answer the questions below:

What are the circumstances that led you to start your business? Or *wanting* to start one?

What is the final outcome you want?

Where would you love to be 12 months from now?

What would life look like on a day-to-day basis when you are running a business you love? What will this *feel* like?

This exercise helps to map out major goals and the way you are going to feel when you get there. Is it a matter of working only three days a week? Get super clear on your Why:

- Do you want more time with your kids?
- Do you want to have enough money in your savings account to help your parents retire?
- Do you want to start a nonprofit?
- Do you want to take more vacations?

When you are working on your Why List, remember the things that enable you to enjoy life. Are you like a lot of women I talk to, who don't take care of themselves? They're so busy taking care of other people, they can't see a time when that will ever end. They are constantly burned out and never have time for themselves. Have you factored self-care into your list? I also want to point out the obvious here (yes, hold the eye-roll for just a moment).

In the beginning, my business WAS my self-care. I was so excited about the business that spending time on it felt as exciting as a two-hour hike in the mountains. So it is more than possible, especially in the beginning, that you will be a little unbalanced. And that's OK. Your business may be your soul-food in the beginning. I say only in the beginning because as entrepreneurship becomes your life, you will have to reign in some self-care strategies (as I did) but that's for another book!

Take your Why list and put it in a place where you're reminded of it all the time, because when you're an entrepreneur, you're going to have good days, and I guarantee you're going to have bad days when you look in the bathroom mirror and think, *I'm giving up. That's it, I'm going back to work. I'm a failure!* When you have those days, you can look at your list and be reminded of your big vision. This is Why you wanted to do this in the first place. This is what I like to call "Your True North Star." This is what you are supposed to be doing. This is the life you have been called to live.

In the next chapter, we are going to look at the no-fluff mindset that will transform your approach to business and life. This is one of my favorite entrepreneurial topics and I will help give you the motivation, the tenacity and grit you need to get started and stay the course.

CHAPTER 5

THE NO-FLUFF MINDSET

Most people are surprised to learn that one of the most important things I teach my students is the power of mindset. Now hang on a second…don't go anywhere just yet!

Being in the research world for many years, I know that flimsy things like "mindset" were scoffed at. Things that couldn't be replicated in a controlled setting of a research study weren't given any weight.

Once I got into the world of entrepreneurship, I suddenly realized how important mindset was, if only out of practicality. Because I had to speak with people on the phone and tell them about my service, my mindset mattered immensely.

If I happened to wake up in a bad mood—maybe I didn't sleep well or was having hormonal mood swings—my sales calls would not go as well. In fact, over the months of making sales calls (a task which even as a shy, introvert, I surprisingly enjoy immensely), I started to realize that the week before my period when I was feeling tired, moody, and less creative, my chances of getting a potential client to say yes to my services were much lower. Because I wasn't in a good mood. And even though I wasn't overtly rude or anything of that nature, I still wasn't as motivated or inspired. Those potential clients were likely picking up on my low energy.

It was only in the trenches of entrepreneurship, making sales calls, and being responsible for my own success, that I realized why so many entrepreneurs focus on mindset and the self-development that you must go through as an entrepreneur to be your best self.

The way you feel affects the way you think. The way you think affects your actions. And your actions affect your business. Simple enough, right? But so many people forget it.

When I was in a bad mood, I would only see the negative in a situation. Maybe I would cast off a client as a bad fit too quickly, or I would get bothered by something that I should have let go. In fact, this negativity bias is something that we all deal with as humans, and I find if we let it get out of control (which can happen when we are not feeling well), it can severely impact our ability to achieve.

This negativity bias is something that is supported by research. In his bestselling book, *The Happiness Advantage*, Shawn Achor talks about the Tetris Experiment, a study of students who played Tetris. After days of playing Tetris, the students started seeing Tetris blocks everywhere they went. When they went to the grocery store, they would imagine stacking the cereal boxes as if in a game of Tetris, for instance.

It's the same way, Achor writes, that lawyers think in "billable hours" at work, and this is behavior that doesn't stop when lawyers go home. In fact, he mentions that many lawyers, who diligently track all their work tasks and activities in 15-minute increments for billing purposes, track their time even during off time (without meaning to)! One lawyer exclaimed he found himself counting each 15-minute increment that he spent talking with his wife about window treatments!

Why is this worth mentioning? Because we can train our brains. Many of us feel that our personalities are our destiny, when we actually have much more control of how we show up in our lives.

The importance of gratitude

It is due to the work of scholars like Shawn Achor that we now know how these cognitive experiments support the concept that what we focus on expands.

If we expand on what we are grateful for, we become happier. If we focus on what we don't have, we'll always be operating from a place of lack. Be assured, you can absolutely train your brain to focus on the positives in your life. This is crucial as an entrepreneur, because you will be more inclined to imagine a positive outcome. Take the time to appreciate all that you have achieved already.

Slow your mind

I used to think that being anxious was just a part of who I was, and that I was slightly more anxious than the normal person. When I started working with my mentor, Scott, in 2019, one of the first things he said to me was, "Sarah, you speak too fast. You're too anxious. By slowing down and stepping into your power and harnessing your goddess energy, you will step up to be the true leader you were meant to be." He said this from a place of love, and I received it.

From that moment on I realized he was right. The more powerful and confident and capable I feel, the more I slow down, and the more that I don't buy into an anxious mindset of *go, go, go.*

It's sort of like the "monkey brain" in Buddhist thought. In university, I was enthralled with Buddhist thinking and they have a theory called the "monkey mind." Our mind is always running, always thinking.

Our minds want to keep us safe, so our minds try to compel us against doing anything aside from the status quo. Anything new is scary. Anything outside our comfort zone is something to be avoided. But in real life, you want to move toward that fear because that is how confidence is grown. Remember, you really have to take action before you're ready.

In fact, if we get really quiet and listen, we can see our minds running amuck with thoughts. As Michael Singer, the author of the *Untethered Soul*, explains it, we have "a mental dialogue going on inside your head that never stops. It just keeps going and going…And if right now you are hearing, 'I don't know what you're talking about. I don't have any voice inside my head!'—that's the voice we're talking about."

The incredible thing about being human is that we can be aware of this chatter with a part of our brain that observes and registers everything that happens to us. This incessant chatter has the job of keeping us safe. Singer points out that to transcend this incessant chatter, we must realize that this chatter isn't necessarily truth. "This world is unfolding and really has very little to do with you or your thoughts." The person you really are— the true you—is the person who is wiser, who is observing the monkey brain. When you can do this, you suddenly have the keys to live a more authentic, certain life.

Tapping into this inner wisdom is also something that's necessary as an entrepreneur. You no longer rely on other people to give you a paycheck; you are 100% responsible for your success in life. The more willing you are to take responsibility for your life, the more successful you will be.

The first step to cultivating the no-fluff mindset is to understand this duality in your mind, and to tap into the deeper inner wisdom we all have.

How many times have you asked someone for advice even though you already knew what to do? As women, we often seek validation through other people's opinions, and if we get really quiet, we often know the answer already. But we don't exactly live in a world that encourages us to tap into this deep inner wisdom because we are trained to be "good girls" and to be obedient.

I teach my students to tap into this deep inner wisdom through making space for contemplative time in their lives. There are a few different ways to do this.

The best way to tap into your inner wisdom (Let's call this voice your True North Star Guide) is meditation. Meditation has been touted for years, across many different cultures and religions, as a way to get closer to the divine. While the form may vary, it is really time you dedicate to slowing down. Meditation is very simple, but not easy. In a world that never slows down, you may feel like a fish out of water, sitting in one place and not having any distractions.

In fact, for those just learning to meditate, it can be helpful to purchase a guided meditation. Starting out with guided meditation can be a little easier to get accustomed to, because you are still listening.

As you get more adept at it though, it can be worthwhile to evolve to just sitting in quiet contemplation. The best way to do this is in a quiet spot (no animals or distractions), with ear plugs and a hoodie (hood pulled up). This is my preferred way to meditate. Twenty minutes a day is ideal, but you can start with just five minutes.

Another great way to have quiet, contemplative time to tap into your True North Star Guide is to journal. Getting out a pen and paper and writing down your stream of consciousness thoughts can be incredibly eye-opening.

This is a practice that I learned from Julia Cameron, who wrote *The Writer's Way* in which she terms these her "morning pages." Write every single morning so you can release worries and anxiety, and start your day off fresh. It is a wonderful ritual to tap into solace.

Another strategy that can work wonders is getting out into nature. At a bare minimum, a walk around your neighborhood will do, but if you can get close to trees and a forest, or water, even better. Detaching ourselves from the connected world (even just for a short time) can be powerful for creating clarity and change in your life.

There are few problems that can't be solved by going to the forest and meditating or taking a quiet walk. You will likely leave with (or be a lot closer to) the answers to whatever problems you are facing.

I also want to mention that this advice is not to replace medical help. If you are persistently anxious or even depressed, it is crucial you seek help. In fact, after going through a particularly tough phase of burnout in my business and wanting to give up, I started talking to a counsellor whom I still speak to every two weeks (this has been for years now). Working from home has meant this was a necessary ingredient for my sanity.

I recommend Better Help[6] a virtual counselling program that has very reasonable rates and very talented counselors.

Let's grow your "I don't care what you think" muscle

The practices above will help you slow down and tap into your deep inner wisdom and that will help you grow what I like to call the "I don't care what you think" muscle. This is a crucial part of the no-fluff mindset.

---

6 https://www.betterhelp.com

You can be brilliant, have the best ideas, and the most marketable skills, but if you don't have the proper mindset, you'll never make a dollar off of all that intelligence and talent.

Don't care what other people think, because when you start your own business, people may judge you, and people may be afraid of you. People may be jealous that you have the audacity to live a life that's unconventional. You get all kinds of interesting reactions from friends and family and coworkers. But I learned to stop caring. It wasn't easy at first, but got much better over time.

The truth of the matter is that other people's opinions do not pay the bills. You are responsible for you and that's that. When you are plagued with feelings of: *But what will they think*? you have to ask yourself why.

Why do you care what they think? It's most likely because—deep down as humans—we want to be accepted. In the early days of human evolution, if we were kicked out of the tribe, we would face certain death. Even though we are no longer living in those harsh times, our brains have not really adapted. We still desperately want to be loved and accepted, so we too often seek this validation from people who don't really matter in the grand scheme of our lives. And sometimes it requires resisting wanting the validation from people close to us if they are not supportive of our dreams.

But you can give *you* the validation you seek. Don't let your brain fool you into thinking you need it from the outside. When we are seeking validation from other people, we are suddenly at their mercy. That makes me feel like a puppet trying to please. But I want to be in control of my life. I want to steer the ship and that means giving myself validation and recognizing when I am seeking validation from others. So next time you're in this situation, try to catch yourself. Slow down for a moment and ask yourself, *Can I give myself the validation I want/need in this moment?*

It's time to remind yourself that tossing aside people's opinions will not lead to certain death, and in fact, by pursuing your dreams in the face of what other people think, you are being a role model for your children, or your nieces and nephews.

What I find funny is that as parents we are so worried about our teenagers doing drugs or getting into trouble, and we all know it usually stems from peer pressure and the need that teenagers have to be accepted. I say to my son often, "Don't care what people think," as I imagine many parents do. Many parents preach it, but in their own lives they are incapacitated by the thoughts and opinions of others.

Another way I force myself to get outside of my comfort zone is to be a role model to my children so I can show them what it's like to live a life without being limited by the opinions of others. In other words, while I'm far from perfect, I try to walk my talk—and that means not caring what other people think.

While it can be well and good to say this on paper, in real life it can be more challenging. In fact, when we are just starting a business, we can be more susceptible to feelings of: *But will I succeed*? Our minds are like a precious garden and those pernicious thoughts are like weeds. To maintain the integrity of your garden and focus your energy and attention where it needs to go (on your business), it is often far easier to simply limit your contact with other people's opinions; and, the best way to do this is to keep the news to only the bare minimum of people.

With my first business I went all out, totally public with everything. Then everyone was watching me when I failed; at least that is the way I felt. I struggled with feelings of humiliation as a result which obviously didn't kill me, but I could have lived without it.

The second time around, I was a little bit smarter. I thought: *This is so important to me, that I'm going to keep it really close to my heart. I'm going to do it quietly.* I did not shout it from the rooftops. I wanted to get a little bit of success before I started to tell people it was a real thing.

So here's my best advice about this (and yes, it's a little counter-intuitive): Don't share your goals with people who are going to judge you and discourage you, because in the very beginning of your business, your mindset is one of your most important assets.

If you let negative people in, their comments are going to chip away at your energy, and in the beginning stages, you need all the energy that you can muster to put toward your business.

Your energy and focus are critically important, and outside factors have the likelihood of bringing you down. Be judicious in who you tell and who you don't. But support is tremendously helpful, so I encourage you to seek out like-minded people, such as the ladies in the previous chapter.

I continually invest in online learning, and there I have met people like me. Quite truly, I met other so-called "misfits" who hated working in an office, who wanted to tell their boss to shove it, who didn't enjoy that type of life. Meeting those people made me realize I'm actually not the only one who almost got fired.

In fact, a lot of entrepreneurs have gotten fired, and it wasn't a sign that they were lazy or ungrateful. It was a sign that they needed something other than the job to motivate them. When I met these other people, I was relieved. I always thought I would never fit in and now I've met people who actually enjoy being in business for themselves. They're self-starters, they're motivated. They are my people.

There are numerous regional business groups, start-up groups, women entrepreneur groups, and some very supportive online communities, too. Facebook groups are a great place to start looking for "your people."

Why your surroundings matter

As I shared in a previous chapter, when I was a teenager, I told my dad that I wanted to be a doctor. He responded, "Sarah being a doctor is really hard. Try to be a teacher." He discouraged me from being a doctor because he had put them up on a pedestal that he felt I could not rise to. Don't get me wrong, my dad loved me like crazy, but he was a very practical man.

When I started working in research, I initially held my father's belief, but the more I talked to doctors and was surrounded by doctors, the veil of mystery lifted. I was riding in the car with my boss, Claire, a family physician, and I told her how I had wanted to be a doctor. When she asked why I stopped, I told her I probably wasn't smart enough.

She responded, "Sarah, 99% of being a doctor is clinical. You learn it and remember it, and that's that." Right there on the spot she demystified the way in which I had believed being a doctor was unattainable. By immersing myself in that environment and having many co-workers who were applying for medical school, I realized I would have been more than able to do this myself. And yes, I considered enrolling in medical school, but decided against it because I was a single mom and medical school is incredibly demanding for many years.

So often, we feel fear around things that are new. Every woman who enrolls in my program goes through a period of overwhelm at learning a new skill. They often doubt they will be able to make any progress. But after just a few weeks in the program, they are throwing around terms like funnels, split-testing, lead magnet, and AOV (average order value) with ease.

As an entrepreneur, you have to be OK with learning new skills and getting outside your comfort zone. As Will Smith says in one of his Instagram videos, "If you can't beat the fear, just do it scared."

There are truly very few things you can't learn if you set your heart and mind to them. You must repeat, "**This is learnable**." Business is not rocket science. Don't fall into the trap of thinking you need to know *everything* before you even get started. You do not need to be an expert, but in time you will become one.

To get started, all you need to know is a little bit more than the person you are helping. That's how I started out. I learned through experimenting over a few months with my own Facebook ads, and then I realized I could also try to help other businesses with theirs. I knew enough to start running ad campaigns for other people. Then, I invested in mentorship to strengthen and expand my skills. Remind yourself daily in the early months of your journey: **This is learnable**.

In a similar vein, don't fall victim to imposter syndrome. Impostor syndrome is that feeling you have inside that you aren't as accomplished as people think you are. That you've gotten where you are by luck rather than talent. You harbor these unfounded feelings that one day you'll be speaking to a group and somebody in the back is going to stand up, ask you a question you can't answer, and then yell, "She's a fake. She doesn't know what she's doing." Now this may sound dramatic, but people have these self-limiting fantasies all the time.

The reality is, we are all learning as we go. No one knows everything. Yes, I've made a whole lot of money by running ads for other people, but it doesn't mean I know everything. If someone tells you they know everything, you can be certain they're lying. Part of my approach is being honest and transparent. If I don't know something, I am not afraid to say, "That's a great question; I know just who to ask to find out." So often we feel like we have to pretend we know it all.

There are ways to learn and to be of service without pretending to be something you're not.

For example, in my program, many of my students are initially worried that they don't have any case studies. They are worried about competing with larger agencies who also run ads and have a proven track record. The reality is that even as a beginner you have value you can provide that the bigger companies cannot. In fact, beginners often have an advantage in how they look at things.

Catrina is a student in my program who got her first project after her client talked to two bigger agencies. He asked her if she was new, and she said she was and added that she would give him the dedicated time, attention and support that he really needed to succeed. He said he was going to take calls with two other larger agencies and did so. He came back to Catrina a week later and said he wanted to proceed to work with her because he knew she would give him the time and attention he really needed to feel heard. So often as beginners we tend to discount our value, but frequently, the people already in the game have too much on their plates anyway.

Paying someone who is too busy was very similar to what I went through with the person who I hired to run my ads. Although I paid her very well ($2K per month), as soon as I joined, she paired me with a junior staff member who was just learning the ropes, so even though I thought I was going to get the talent who had created the advertising for *New York Times* best-sellers, I was really getting someone brand new to the game.

This happens to companies who work with advertising agencies all the time. This is exactly why I have been able to teach hundreds of women to provide a truly high-quality service and succeed right out of the gate as beginners.

Now, back to the person I hired, as I want to make one more crucial point. I was paying her team $2K a month to run my ads, and one day I looked into my Facebook ad account (where we schedule and run the ads) and saw what she was doing. I thought, *This is not rocket science. She's doing very simple advertising. I can absolutely do that.* At that time, I was a bit surprised that people paid her $2K a month to do that and clearly, she was very successful, so there must have been many of her clients who were successful and selling something way better than I was! (Yes, you can have the best advertising strategies in the world, but if you are not selling a desirable product that meets a market need, you won't succeed—that's what I learned the hard way.) At first, I was in awe of her ability, but just three months later, I was setting up online ads like nobody's business. I respected what she did, but also knew I was capable of it.

You need to be in a business where you get paid for what you know, not for the number of hours it takes you to fulfill the requests. That was something that I learned from the ads manager I hired to work on my advertising. She was clearly getting paid for what she knew and not how long it took her to do it, because the tasks didn't take much time.

You can actually learn the skills of an ads manager in about six to 12 weeks. The rest of the learning is on-the-job training. It's kind of like when you go to college: you spend four years getting your degree, then you get into the workplace and realize there's so much more you need to learn from the school of real life. I'm still learning about advertising every day as the industry evolves.

You don't need to know everything

You can make a huge contribution to people's businesses if you are just a few steps ahead of them, and you're dedicated to helping them find a great solution. Get comfortable with not knowing everything and understand that just because you don't know everything, it doesn't mean that you're an imposter. (And here's a secret: no matter how much success you have, you will still have moments when you feel like an imposter.)

Human beings are evolving creatures and we learn every single day—and no one in the world has everything figured out. There's no ads manager in the world who knows everything. There's no *anyone* who knows everything. The sooner you accept that you can make a contribution, as in right now, the better and faster you'll be able to succeed.

Don't wait for the perfect time

It's literally never going to happen. Just like it's never a great time to pay taxes, it's never the right time to start your business. It's like when you're dating and you're waiting for the perfect guy or girl, they never show up. Just accept that now is better than never and get started.

Be careful not to get held back by perfectionism. I have seen women in my program get so fixated on things being perfect, that they stall their progress and take double or triple the amount of time it has to take, just because they had this fixed mindset that everything has to be perfect.

You need to be okay with winging it. I heard this quote along the lines of "Entrepreneurs are the type of people who jump out of a building and then build the parachute on the way down." This is true!

For even more inspiration around entrepreneurship and building it as you go, I highly recommend the book, *Winging It*, by Emma Isaacs. It's extremely enlightening.

Show up

There is an expression that "ideas are cheap," and that's true. You can have the best ideas in the world, but if you don't implement, you won't create change.

Instead of perfection and mastery, focus on showing up every day. Show up, do the work, put your time into your business and treat it like a business before it actually is a business. Then there is a much higher likelihood of success. Stop analyzing, just show up. One of my students on a call yesterday said to me, "Sarah, I'm really worried I'm not going to be able to do this."

I responded, "You absolutely can do it. It's not a question of if you can or can't. The question is, what are you going to focus on?" If you focus your energy on *Oh, I can't do this*, you're putting your nervous system into fight or flight mode all the time and you'll be panicked and worried. That saps the energy you could be spending productively on your business. Then sadly, because you're consumed with that, you're not going to learn as quickly and you're going to stunt your progress.

One of the things that was so crucial when starting my business was that I didn't analyze. I didn't overthink. I just did. Say to yourself, over and over: *If it's meant to be, it's up to me*. That is the truth.

Radical responsibility

By reading my story, you know that I have failed a lot. You also know that things didn't come easily to me. In fact, many people in my position, with so much business failure, would have given up (and for a while I did).

Something that I've practiced, which is integral to success as an entrepreneur, is something called "radical responsibility." It's the idea that we are all responsible for our lives. While we cannot always control the things that happen (sometimes bad things just happen that are far out of our control), we can absolutely control how we respond in a situation.

One of the most important things we can do in bad situations, is to ask ourselves, *What can I learn from this*?

Remember the research institute I worked at and the grant they didn't get. That was a really sucky situation; I'd blown it. I couldn't hide under a rock for the rest of my life; instead, I asked myself, *What can I learn from this situation*? I (obsessively) became a really good researcher and ironically ended up being the person on my next team who submitted all the grants because I had such an epic failure the first time. I learned how to write the grants and I would have them completed a week in advance, which is extremely hard.

My father passed away a week after we had gotten into a big argument. He was hard on me at times and that argument was an example of that. In my 20s, I was more stubborn than I am now, and I couldn't predict how I would feel after he passed away.

But I learned from the experience of my father's death—and specifically having a major disagreement so soon before his passing—that I can beat myself up until the end of time, or I can accept that I was human. I was in my 20s, and that experience humbled me into a better person.

We all have control over how we interpret the events that happen to us. We can choose to play the victim and stay stuck in a world where we have no control, or we can take control of the narrative and ask ourselves: *What can I glean from this situation? What can I learn and how can I improve for next time*?

This mindset is what separates children from true adults—of course I don't have to tell you that some grownups act like children all the time!

Radical responsibility is the differentiator between those who succeed and those who do not. The responsible ones are the self-starters, the people who will succeed at all costs, who are obsessed with their vision. You know them when you see them. They are the hustlers. And I don't mean hustlers in a way that glorifies busy; I mean it in terms of their level of commitment. They are completely driven.

The person who is radically responsible takes more responsibility in a situation than most people would, because they understand that no one is going to save them. There will be no knight in shining armor riding up to rescue them. This person isn't deterred by failure. Instead, they learn and then do better.

I've had sales calls during which I've been embarrassed. I didn't come off like I had my act together and I said something stupid which came across as incompetent. After I hung up the phone, I would do as my dad always said to me, "You've got to pick yourself up, dust yourself off, and try again." I gave myself permission to fail and be a beginner and learn.

People are so afraid of moving into this life of entrepreneurship because they're afraid they're going to fail.

The truth is you *are* going to fail. No doubt, you're going to have some mortifying moments. An entrepreneur asks herself: *What can I take away from this? How can I make this better*? Keep moving forward because you're going to learn as you go. What's the worst that can happen? It's usually far worse in our minds than it actually is in real life.

As Cher said in an interview, "Until you're ready to look foolish, you'll never have the possibility of being great."

Recognize the ego's voice and tell it to be quiet, and go away. The ego says, *I have to be the ultimate expert. I need to have five degrees hanging on the wall and know everything perfectly*. Getting over the ego is getting over yourself. Nobody knows everything. We're all just showing up, doing our best, asking great questions, caring about people. If you care about helping people, you will find success because when you're truly invested in a client, success will happen.

A word on risk

The reality is that business involves risk. In fact, life involves risk. It's a risk to take a bus or drive a car. It's a risk to walk across the street. While often small, there are risks in every part of our lives. It's a part of the human experience. In fact, to go to the extreme, it's a risk to stay locked up in your house out of fear of danger, as that puts you at risk of poor health.

No one ever fully lived if they were always dragged down by fear and anxiety. We can get into a really miserable space when we feel crippled by self-doubt, and as if we can't do what we really want to do and be who we really want to be because of fear. If we are always avoiding what we want because of fear and anxiety, we are not really living a full life.

So, what do we do? We map out what is meaningful to us. We identify what we really believe in and value. Is it freedom? Independence? Family? Helping people? Creativity? Making money?

And when we've identified what matters to us and what we value, we take calculated risks to get there. That's what makes us feel truly alive (whether we succeed or not!). The feeling that we did everything we could to move in the direction of our dreams, despite the risks.

If you're reading this book, one of the values that you may have is to own your own business for any number of reasons. So it makes sense to take the risks to get there.

Sure, you could start a business and fail. But people rarely consider they could start a business and really succeed. And how would that change your life?

How resourceful are you?

If you're reading this book, you're probably far more resourceful than you're giving yourself credit for. Many of us have been through countless situations where our first thought was, *How will I get through this*? Yet we did. I often ask the women in my group to "meditate on your resourcefulness." Try this exercise to strengthen your mindset:

- Get out a piece of paper.
- Write down a list of challenges you overcame in your life. Everyone in my class and everyone reading this book has overcome challenges.
- Read through your list. Did you put yourself through school? Survive a divorce? Have a miracle baby? At the time you probably didn't even know how you were going to overcome those challenges. And here you are today, wiser and stronger.
- At the end of each week, go back and reread your list and you will see just how strong and accomplished you are. Use this swipe file for a confidence boost whenever you need it.

Human beings are incredibly resourceful. As long as your guiding philosophy is to provide a great service to your client, even if you don't know all the answers, you will always find a solution. This continued practice will turn into a belief and that belief will push your ego out of the way.

When you put all of these pieces together …

- *Start* with your Why. What are your values?
- Develop the "I don't care what you think" muscle.
- Repeat to yourself, *I can learn this. It's OK not knowing today. I will gain confidence as I go.*
- Show up and do the work.
- Have faith in yourself.
- Surround yourself with the right people.
- Take radical responsibility for yourself.
- Understand risk is a part of a life well-lived.
- *Remember* your Why.

You have developed the no-fluff mindset.

CHAPTER 6

WHO DO YOU WANT TO BE?

Do you sit at your desk, daydreaming about being a business owner instead of a support tech? Do you find yourself fantasizing about Caribbean vacations while you are folding the laundry? Do you imagine yourself driving a Jaguar instead of a minivan?

Do you play that "If I Had the Time" game? If I had the time, I'd be at every one of my kiddos' soccer games. If I had the time, I'd go to the spa and get regular massages.

How about the "If I Had the Money" game? If I had the money, I'd move into a bigger house, If I had the money, I'd put the kids in a better school. If I had the money, I could pay off my debt.

Who is the person who can make all this happen? Do you believe it could be you? Daydreaming is a very useful exercise. It is a peek into who you would really like to be.

Take a minute and indulge in a little visualization

You are going to imagine your life the way it would be if you could snap your fingers and make it happen—just like that! Close your eyes, and in your mind's eye, look down and describe what you are wearing, where you are standing. Is your family with you? What are you doing? Are you inside or outside? What is the weather like?

By focusing on *WHO* you want to be, the *how* of getting there will unfold for you. If your daydream exercise didn't include getting a 30-years-of-service plaque from your employer, it may be time to consider starting your own business.

Try out some "I am" statements to help you figure out your "who." Here are some idea starters, but have fun with this and come up with your own.

- I am a mom who has quality time to spend with my kids, not just shoveling dinner into their mouths and packing them off to bed.
- I am in great shape and I fit going to the gym into my schedule several times a week.
- I am in a healthy relationship. I have plenty of time and energy to focus on my partner.
- I am taking a dream vacation at least twice a year.

Don't just focus on a money number, like I want to earn $10K a month. Focus on Why you want that. How will your life change with that income? Will you be saving for the down payment on a house? Getting a dependable car? Who else will be touched by what you do?

We used "snapping your fingers" for imagining who we want to be, but we know it's not that easy, right? It takes tenacity and consistency. You need to keep showing up every day to create the Who you know you can become.

Your Who and your Why will be very closely tied to one another. A big, big Why for me was really examining who I wanted to be in the world. I knew I didn't want to be a 9-to-5 worker. Those are important jobs that need to get done, but not by me. I wanted to show my children a different way of living because I wasn't happy with the 9-to-5 path.

I asked myself: *What kind of mother am I, if I resent my life, and I'm not happy with my job, and I'm not able to see my children?* Sooner or later, the kids are going to pick up on that dissatisfaction. As an entrepreneur, I feel a sense of pride when I reflect on how I make more money now than in my traditional job I went to college for. I easily earn more each month than I used to make in an entire year. Now, I can truly be a role model to my children.

"Entrepreneur" is a little bit of a buzzword right now, but society still discourages us from taking the risk. Other people can be very judgmental when they see us struggling. Instead of encouraging us to keep going, they are quick to say, "Oh, come on, grow up, just get a job, go to work."

If you have the calling to do something different, that urge will keep coming up again and again. If your inner voice keeps speaking up, *Maybe I could work for myself. Maybe I can be creative and get paid well for it,* that voice isn't going to go away.

Maybe we're born this way. My grandparents and parents didn't have the choice, but despite how hard I worked at the regular life, I wasn't satisfied until I tried my hand at entrepreneurship. My brother, Aaron, couldn't resist either. He went to military school and got a government job. He and his wife worked for the government for years, but they, too, listened to that voice in their head. They both quit their jobs, moved to the Caribbean and started a business. From there, they went to Victoria, BC and opened a string of bakeries. Maybe it's in our blood.

If you have the entrepreneur's calling, it is worth pursuing. You deserve to enjoy your life. Who do you really want to be in this world? Do you want to be the person who didn't take chances and played by the rules up until the day they died? Or do you want to be the person who actually has the courage and the drive to try for a satisfying life, the person who is bold enough to try, even if it means losing it all? Because you just might actually gain a whole lot more than you lose along the way. Playing by the rules is just not that inspiring.

The time is never perfect. The time is never perfect for having kids, or starting a business, or buying a house, or taking a vacation. If you wait for the perfect time, you'll be on your deathbed with regrets.

Talk about bad timing: The pandemic changed everything. One day, we're slogging along in jobs that are *meh*, and the next day, we're stuck at home, missing the job we complained about all the time.

Some women lost their jobs and are either waiting to get called back, or actively looking for another position. A disproportionate number of women are handling the burden of homeschooling and working remotely. According to a McKinsey report, nearly two million women are considering leaving the workforce[7].

The pandemic has also been a time of self-examination and taking stock. People are saying to themselves, *I've got to do something to earn a living, I'm stuck in the house, now is the time to try something new.* According to *The Wall Street Journal*, new business applications have skyrocketed during the pandemic[8]. People are getting inspired during the most frightening and challenging of times.

People are pivoting in two ways: they have the "nothing left to

7 https://www.mckinsey.com/featured-insights/diversity-and-inclusion/women-in-the-workplace

8 https://www.wsj.com/articles/is-it-insane-to-start-a-business-during-coronavirus-millions-of-americans-dont-think-so-11601092841

lose" mindset to start a new business, or they have the "now that I have time on my hands" motivation to take the first steps to a long-held dream, like writing a book, or learning a new skill.

What about you? Is it time to start living the life you've dreamed about?

Once I started seeing consistent success with my business, I wanted to share what I had learned. I was so excited, I wanted other people to be inspired to reach their dreams, too. Remember my love of teaching? I started mentoring some women who wanted to learn how to have Ads Management businesses also.

Two of the women I mentor are perfect examples of the pandemic pivot. Lauren had what she called "a super stressful job" as director of finance for a tech company. She got laid off in April and started working with me to learn how to become an ads manager. By August, she had started her own digital marketing agency and had three signed contracts worth a minimum $6K each (and many clients renew month and month again.) That fast.

Starting your own business is definitely a confidence builder. As Lauren says, "My family is impressed, my friends are proud of me. So, if you feel that voice calling you, just go for it, you won't regret it." Lauren is working half the hours that she used to, and is bringing in $10K a month.

Whitney is another mentee. She was furloughed from her hospitality job during the pandemic. After devoting herself to learning something new, she had her first client within two weeks. (That fast!) She has no plans to go back to the type of work she did before, with a schedule that required her to spend nights and weekends away from her family.

Do their stories look exciting or scary to you? A lot of people think they are risk-averse, but really, they've just been conditioned to accept some risks and not others. What if somebody said to you, "Invest $100K and spend four to six years learning some general knowledge that will qualify you for a job that pays maybe $60K or $80K a year. You'll get home exhausted every night and get to take two weeks off a year. Oh, and you'll spend the next 20 years paying off the debt."

That tells the story of a traditional education and the traditional life, and everybody is OK with that kind of risk.

Or what about the risk of buying a house? Most people don't realize the interest on a home loan can be greater than the principal. You are paying more for the privilege of going into debt than you are for your house. And everybody is OK with that kind of risk, too. People will congratulate you when you sign your name to a 30-year mortgage, but scoff if you say you want to start your own business.

Mandy is another mentee who quickly identified her Who and her Why. She had earned her bachelor's and master's degrees and had been working as an English teacher for many years. She realized one day, "I was always available for everyone else's children and not my own … so when Sarah's opportunity presented itself, I jumped on board with enthusiasm." Learning a skill that would enable Mandy to be her own boss was worth more to her, she claims, than the thousands and thousands of dollars she invested in her formal education. When Mandy first started her new business, she was a self-described "technophobe."

I worked with her to recognize that fear of technology is a mindset that can be overcome. It's not that hard to learn technical processes. She's a really wonderful example of someone who came into the program, learned the materials, and implemented them. She's now making anywhere between $15,000 to $17,000 a month and has brought on a team member to assist her.

One thing a lot of business books don't tell you is that by going through the process of learning and launching your business, you will develop a sense of confidence that doesn't come with a traditional education. You will be learning something new every day, whether it is a software skill, or an efficient way of outsourcing. With each challenge you face and conquer, your armor of self-confidence gets stronger.

Here's an example: For most of my life I was shy and uncertain and lacked confidence. While it's likely tied to my "don't get too big for your britches" upbringing, who knows really why it started. I was anxious and worried, and often questioned my decisions, even my own opinions.

Once I got into entrepreneurship my confidence began to grow. I took one leap of faith (starting the raw food training program), then another leap (getting on video), then another leap (teaching a class). Bit by bit, my confidence was built through showing up and serving others.

When you are called to make an impression in the world, you suddenly realize people are looking up to you and counting on you. That step-by-step progress allowed me to become a more confident person.

While you might not have confidence from day one, I can attest to the fact—again and again—that confidence is built in the doing. It's not built by contemplation or observation. It's built through taking action **every single day**. Through these actions, like a baby taking their first steps, you build the muscle of entrepreneurship and of confidence.

One of my biggest confidence-builders has also been working with wonderful mentors and surrounding myself with people with similar goals. This has given me the courage to move forward on the days I didn't quite believe in myself.

Overall, entrepreneurship builds confidence for those of us who crave it, because we are living the truest versions of ourselves. No more hiding. No more pretending we are happy with the status quo. We are newly dedicated to forging our own paths and defining what freedom and impact means to us. Living truer to who we really are makes us more confident and certain.

Spend some time thinking about your Who and your Why. Then write them down and place them somewhere that you can see them every day. It may be on the inside of your medicine cabinet or on your home screen. When you lose your motivation or have a particularly challenging day, you will look back at your Who and Why statements and be reminded of your goals.

I've included some practical tips to keep you organized and focused on your new business path.

1. Treat your business idea like a job.
2. Do at least three things every day that will move your business forward.
3. Use a calendar to write down tasks in addition to appointments—even if your task for the day is researching a business name or your competition.
4. As you get busier, use a project management tool like Trello or Asana to electronically manage your to-do list.
5. Arrange childcare, not just for date night, but for hours you dedicate to your business.

CHAPTER 7

DON'T GET LOCKED INTO THE WORK-FROM-HOME PRISON: THE MLM TRAP

Oh sure, they make promises. They talk a good talk. They suck you in with free samples of makeup or a magical diet supplement. Then they drive you to a pep rally where everybody acts like a 4-year-old on a sugar high. High-energy, high-earners, skip across the stage in a frenzy only matched by a summertime tent revival in the south. Buy some product. Tell your friends. Make a million dollars!

You wonder why isn't everybody doing this, why isn't everybody making an additional $10K a month without leaving the house? Six months later, and $3K deeper into debt, you've figured it out.

Multi-level Marketing (MLM) is a venture that one in 13 of us has given a try. You might as well move to Hollywood in hopes of becoming a movie star, or maybe pan for gold in hopes of becoming rich. Now don't get me wrong, there are some high earners in the MLM business, but they are rare, and they work at their business 24 hours a day. If you are someone who wants to see their children before high school graduation, or maybe have a date night with your husband, that is not the path for you.

Nine out of 10 people confess they actually lost money in the MLM journey. According to a report released by the Federal Trade Commission, "less than 1% of MLM participants profit. MLM makes even gambling look like a safe bet in comparison[9]."

Another drawback is the need to tap into your friends and family network in order to generate sales for your MLM products. Revenue is dependent on your downlines. So, if they don't perform, your revenue goes down.

You're also severely capped because your friends and family get tired of you pestering them after a few months. And then you have to start doing curiosity-based marketing on Facebook, which means you post things like, "Wow, I lost 10 pounds. Guess what I'm drinking."

MLMs are very attractive because of the low barrier to entry. "Get started for just 97 bucks a month." I've done it too. I've fallen victim to these MLMs. In 2017, I invested in Monat vegan hair products. This is not your grandmother's Amway. Their website features a highly produced slow-motion video of gorgeous, long-haired Millennials, literally skipping through stunning landscapes. They use lots of enticing language such as: "opportunity," "market partners," and "VIP program."

I went all out and spent $1,100 on the big master pack because I was determined to succeed at that business no matter what. I didn't sell a thing. But I had enough shampoo for two years! The trap is that it's low barrier and seemingly low risk. Women think they can just approach friends and family to buy the products and become distributors. But I think what happens—at least what happened for me—is that I became filled with a sense of shame. I began to feel like it wasn't

[9] https://www.ftc.gov/sites/default/files/documents/public_comments/trade-regulation-rule-disclosure-requirements-and-prohibitions-concerning-business-opportunities-ftc.r511993-00008%C2%A0/00008-57281.pdf

a business I could really feel proud of because (another) problem with MLMs is that the products themselves are overpriced to entice people into becoming distributors (and get a distributor discount.)

It was hard for me to go up to my friend and say, "Hey, buy the shampoo. It's the best shampoo I've ever used. Oh, it's only $80 for a bottle of shampoo. Oh, well, if you want to actually pay a more reasonable rate then become a distributor, and then you'll get a half-decent rate." I felt slimy doing that. It just wasn't my style.

I'm not saying there's anything wrong with selling MLM. If you truly believe in the product, and you are the kind of person with the time and drive it takes to be among the less than 1% who can make a profit at an MLM, I encourage you to follow that path.

I have heard the good thing about MLM is that the social community is pretty great. Just consider the whole picture before you make even the smallest investment. You will probably need to have parties, just like your mother's generation had Tupperware parties. That is night and weekend work.

There are the additional costs of things like the gas money it takes to drive around visiting prospects, and traveling expenses for attending company events. How much will you have to pay a babysitter so you can make it to all these appointments? The cost of cell phones, computers, printing, and even renting rooms for sales and recruitment events are all paid by the distributors (you) and not reimbursed by the company. The odds of making any sort of profit are 1 in 3,922, so if you're truly looking to make more money and more freedom, it's not the best business to start.

Reality Check: WFH businesses

At least MLMs will get you out of the house. Let's look at some other businesses that will keep you locked in the house and glued to your keyboard. I've researched the average income for some of these positions, and just like MLMs, there will always be outliers who are earning six figures, but even average salaries can take years to reach.

Virtual assistant	:	minimum wage — $25 an hour at expert level
Blogger	:	average $27 an hour, top earners $43 an hour
Etsy shop owner	:	extremely time-consuming, most earn a few hundred a month
Drop shipper/Shopify	:	average $72 per customer (this is really optimistic – most eCommerce stores fail and take an incredible amount of startup money)
Copywriter	:	$27 per hour average
Social media manager	:	$24 per hour average
Bookkeeper	:	$26 per hour average
Transcriptionist	:	$15 per hour average

When you read this list, you are likely to say, "That doesn't look too bad. $27 an hour is pretty decent; after all, that's $56K a year." The average American earns $31K and the average Canadian earns $55K. But let's look a little more deeply at those numbers.

The annual salary is based on 2,080 work hours. This means that you would have to actually have 40 billable hours a week. That's an 8-hour day of doing nothing but writing, posting, or transcribing. As a freelancer, you have to *get* the work before you can *do* the work. That can be an additional 15 hours a week networking, having meetings, writing proposals, doing the invoicing, and taking phone calls. 780 hours. Would you like to take a one-week vacation? Subtract 40 hours of billable time.

Now you're looking at $34K before expenses. Computers, cell phones, printers, Zoom accounts, travel, subscription services to places like Upwork or publicity.com, internet, training, advertising, and on and on. If you're being paid by the hour, you're going to be severely limited in the capacity to grow your business and the ability to leave your house. When you are starting out, the only way to compete is to lower your rates, which then means that you don't have enough margin to outsource any of your tasks.

The people who excel despite the odds are the ones with a deep passion and drive for the particular thing they are doing. It could be furniture-making or blogging. The people who get the most press are not necessarily making the most money. Many businesses based on personality—influencers, brand ambassadors, coaches—are not breaking even, have other income sources, or have invested hundreds of thousands of dollars. There are also very few overnight sensations. Getting to the higher end of the earning spectrum can take 10 to 15 years!

Not everyone has a passion or calling. And that is not only OK, but very common. Don't be down on yourself because you don't hear angelic voices "calling" you to make children's clothing. You can choose the way you earn a living based on your financial goals and the type of tasks you enjoy doing. Introverts are not going to be drawn to MLM, but the self-employed lifestyle can suit them perfectly.

The two skill sets you *will* need though, are self-discipline and a willingness to take responsibility. *You* are going to be the boss and making the decisions.

Start with what you know—or something you like to do or find easy— something that your friends and coworkers ask you to do for them. And here is a really important point worth repeating: You don't have to know everything about your topic.

Let's say you're on LinkedIn all the time or love to whip up an Excel spreadsheet (multi-tab with color coding, please). You only need to know a little bit more than someone who is just starting out. If you look at a task someone else is doing and say to yourself, *I could do that*, or *I could do that better*, there's every likelihood you can.

The next thing you want to ask yourself is, *Would someone pay me to do this, so they don't have to*? Don't get hung up on, I *would never pay for this.* There are people who would never dream of washing their own car or homeschooling their kids or doing their own hair, and there are multi-million-dollar businesses based on just those things. The proof is in the pudding for me now. Three years after saying "I can do that," I'm teaching people to do the same thing: become highly paid Ads Managers *just* because I had the courage to start.

In the next chapter, we will be exploring more ways to create practical profits from skills that can be learned quickly and easily.

CHAPTER 8

PRACTICAL PROFITS FROM IN-DEMAND SKILLS

"When you love what you do, you'll never work a day in your life." That quote, or one like it, has been attributed to everyone from Marc Anthony to Oprah Winfrey. What if you don't *love* what you do? What if you don't *know* what you love? What if you don't know what you *want* to do?

There are two things you *do* know: What you are doing right now isn't making you happy (or making you enough money), and you still have bills to pay.

Have you said any of these things to yourself?

- I really want a business.
- I really want to be my own boss.
- I want to work hard for myself, but I don't know what to do.

I asked myself all those questions and many more. For years and years, I would sit in coffee shops brainstorming with my mom and grandma about, "What business can we do?" We called them our pow-wow sessions and would say things like, "Let's do our research.

Do we sell things on eBay?"

Then my mom and grandma would actually go out and test it. My grandma would buy a whole bunch of stuff and then sell it on eBay, and my mom would go to the post office with all the packages. We were all on this mission to figure out what could we really do to bring in more money.

My mom recently said to me, "I always knew this would happen for you. I knew this is why I pushed you all the time." She and grandma have always been my biggest supporters. My grandma has since passed away, but I still carry the business confidence she gave me.

There are some people who have to follow their calling because they are exceptionally good at it. Writers, salespeople, life coaches. But maybe you're like me. I was really kind of flexible. I could do anything as long as it paid me well enough. I was able to stay home with my son. I was able to help people. I could make a contribution if all those check boxes were marked off. It didn't really matter how I applied my skills, I just wanted to be practical.

Making money online is not a mirage. It's a reality

In the last chapter we talked about the stay-at-home prisons that don't work for most people. A lot of them involve online businesses, but the good news is you *can* earn money online. You just have to be more discerning about the business you choose.

Start by looking at your skills. What are you good at? I always loved writing. As a kid, I wanted to be a writer. I've always really loved helping people in university. So I thought, well, maybe I'll be a social worker. Do you like helping people? Do you like being creative? If so, then those are skills that can be applied in many different ways.

One of the highest profit ways is to help people behind the scenes of their business. You can be highly creative and also get paid well in return if you focus on the right skill.

If you want freedom and flexibility, the right type of business is one that you can run from anywhere. If you want to work from home, fine. If you prefer to travel, as long as you have a strong Wifi signal, you have location freedom.

The right type of business pays well enough so that you're not always running around like a chicken with its head cut off. You've got some time to take a breather and think: *What are my priorities today? What does my week look like*? Those are all crucial ingredients as well for the right type of business.

Need vs. want

You need a skill that can demonstrate a potential return on investment for a client. You also need a skill that's not paid by the hour so that you can retain control over your schedule. Learn a valued skill that people are willing to pay for. Does anybody really *need* another shampoo? Does anybody *need* personal coaching or massage? Those things are nice but look for the needs over the wants and you will have a steadier client base and income stream.

What does everyone want to do right now? Everyone wants to start a business. What is something that you could contribute to the business world that would be of value? The ads they *need* to market their business.

Like so many other people, I spent years chasing a passion-based business that did not prove profitable for me. I changed my attitude and decided, *I'm going to get really practical and learn a valued skill that people are willing to pay for*. Then in a backward way, I actually found my passion through helping people with that skill. So it's really just about getting practical and figuring out what people are really paying for.

When we identify what makes for a skill that's in high demand and pays well, then it can build pretty fast. I know with many passion-based businesses, people are used to hearing things like, "Oh, it takes seven or 10 years to be an overnight success."

I remember when I was failing in my first business, that statement was like a balm for my worried soul, because I would convince myself that I just needed more time. But the funny thing is, when I learned an in-demand skill that paid well, the success came fast. I had a handful of clients in just a few months. Now, I have pushed back against the philosophy that it takes seven years for an overnight success.

If you want to be the next Tony Robbins or Marie Forleo, it's going to take you a long time. It takes years to establish that kind of rapport and earn hundreds of thousands of dollars.

Behind the scenes

A lot of people say to me, "I don't want to be a mini-celebrity. I don't want to be doing Facebook Lives." Not everybody is cut out to be in front of the camera. There is a lot more to it than turning the phone camera on yourself and hitting "record."

The great thing about being an Ads Manager is that it's completely behind the scenes. You can run the business with your laptop and your phone. You don't need to make public appearances or organize parties. This business is very well-suited to introverts.

You can provide the service to the people who *want* to be the next Tony Robbins, Marie Forleo, or Gary V. *And* you're getting paid while you're behind the scenes.

Be your own boss

When we work for someone else, they can say to us, "If you don't like it, lump it." Whereas the nice thing about being an entrepreneur is if you take on a client that you feel isn't really a good fit, you have the freedom to end the contract. You have the freedom to pick and choose the clients that you really want to work with. Or not. I've talked to potential clients and I thought, *I'm not that inspired to work on this product. I don't really feel like it.* You have more control over how you're making money, and who you're making it with, so that the time you are working feels more enjoyable.

Part-time work for full-time pay

Some people are ready to jump into their new venture full-time. They've been laid off or are taking a gap year. Other people want to start as a side gig to provide an additional income stream with the potential to move into their new venture on a full-time basis gradually.

In the first month, because there's a heavier setup, we typically devote about 10 to 12 hours per client, per month, because we're doing some important, foundational set-up pieces.

A client will typically sign a three-month contract at minimum (many stay years). For each month thereafter for ad management, it's usually about five to seven hours per month. So if you're looking to make $10K per month and you want to work part-time hours, you need five clients to hit that goal.

When you're an entrepreneur, it is not like you're walking into the office, clocking in your time and then clocking out. Every three to four months, I go through a little bit of a busier season when I'm doing client deliverables, and also I'm doing calls with clients. Then what happens is we get a new client and it goes back to normal.

Obviously, entrepreneurship is not 20 hours a week. Some weeks are busy and then some weeks are really light. Still, you are working part-time hours for full-time pay. If you want to work 20 to 25 hours per week, you can make $10K per month. If you work it full time, $20K per month is a reasonable target. And, if you want to move beyond that, hiring a team can be an excellent way to start hitting anywhere from $25K to $60K months and beyond.

CHAPTER 9

MAKE MONEY ONLINE

We've talked about some of the pitfalls of business opportunities that can be found online. Let's talk about the upside.

The overhead is very low

If you have a computer, internet, and a phone, you can start your online business. As mentioned previously, one of my clients felt she was not that computer savvy before she started, but within a few weeks, she was perfectly comfortable at the keyboard.

Everything you need to know about an online business is learnable. One of the things that holds many people back from becoming an entrepreneur is a fear of technology.

Trust me, you don't need to know enough to work at the Mac Genius Bar, and everything you do need to know can be picked up pretty quickly. Don't worry, you won't break the computer or blow up the internet. It's even nearly impossible to publish something online accidentally. Unlike printing, if you do make a mistake, you can fix it with a few keystrokes. You can unpublish as quickly as you publish.

You do not need the most expensive computer on the market with the largest screen. Yes, you can run your business on a laptop. I worked on a crummy, old laptop my first year. In fact, my first real gift to myself in my first year of business was a new computer—but I didn't need it to start the business.

Here are all the things you *won't* need with an online business

- No employee benefits—no vacation, health, taxes, or payroll
- No rent for a brick-and-mortar office
- No transportation cost—no commuting or monthly parking fees
- No inventory—no investment or cost of storage and shipping
- Minimal business insurance (This is optional, although I do recommend errors and omissions liability insurance, which is reasonably priced)
- No business clothes. Even for Zoom calls, we only have to look good from the waist up
- No entertainment costs: Goodbye 3-martini lunches! Even the cost of buying lunch out can add up to hundreds of dollars a month
- No accountants or employee payroll and benefits vendors to pay
- No full-time childcare

Plus, you can write off a portion of your home as an office. Check the local tax laws where you live.

Hit the road

You don't even have to work from home if you don't want to. The online business environment is perfect for the growing trend in digital nomads. It's estimated these remote workers number in the tens of millions worldwide. These are the people living the van life or traveling around the world. With a laptop and Wifi, your business can travel where you do. Gone are the days of driving around, aiming your laptop out the window to get a signal. Most cell services come with hotspots now, so you can be online almost anywhere. The majority of women I directly mentor are moms who need to stay in one place for good deal of the year, but like knowing they can take a quick getaway when they want.

Home sweet home

Not all of us want to hit the open road; we find our freedom by spending more time at home. We decide when to get up, which hours we want to work, and when to take breaks. Not everyone is cut out for a 9-to-5 workday. Studies have shown that productivity differs from individual to individual.

The average North American and European worker is only productive for less than three hours per day[10]. For some people that is early morning; for others, mid-afternoon is their peak performance time. If you are a morning person who has company-mandated meetings three times a week at 9:00 a.m., you are missing out on your best times to produce.

This means, when you have the flexibility to work when you want, you get more accomplished in a shorter period of time. Yes, it is possible to work less and earn more.

---

[10] https://www.inc.com/melanie-curtin/in-an-8-hour-day-the-average-worker-is-productive-for-this-many-hours.html

Choose your circle

How many of your 9-to-5 job complaints were about your boss or your coworkers? How many times were you forced to chip in for a birthday, retirement, or shower present for someone who you really didn't like, or even know that well? Did you leave the office wondering if that guy really was trying to sabotage you? Did you watch other, less-qualified people get the promotion you felt you deserved? Well, those days are over when you own an online business.

You will still have to deal with other people, but you get to choose who, and for how long. Ads management clients stay anywhere from 3 months to many years. All of your interaction will be by phone, video chat, email, or some other electronic method.

This keeps a personal distance that you don't have with regular jobs. You won't be drawn into office politics or have to listen to uncomfortable family dramas. An online business is ideal for introverts.

For people who do crave more social interaction, consider joining a co-working space, which number approximately 19,000 worldwide and are growing at a rate expected to reach 25,000 by 2025 [11]. Not only will you get your much-needed social interaction, chances are, you will pick up new clients when they find out what you do.

---

[11] https://teamstage.io/coworking-statistics/

CHAPTER 10

NAVIGATING THE ONLINE LABYRINTH

Let's talk about the confusion of the online landscape. If you are reading this book, chances are you have already experienced some of this. You are looking for a business, and you are a logical, reasonable person who is doing your due diligence. You are researching.

The way Facebook ads work and the way social platforms with advertising work is, once we show an interest in one thing, we get inundated with more of the same, and more, and more, and more.

For instance, when someone initially shows an interest in starting a business, they will explore some websites. Facebook catches on that they are interested in starting a business.

Then what happens is information overload.

You start getting targeted with all kinds of ads for business ideas. You'll see an ad or wind up on a landing page with copy that reads, "Start this Shopify business. I started five years ago and now I'm a millionaire!" Well, no wonder. You started five years ago; the whole landscape has gotten far more crowded since then.

The way social media is designed—and the way the ads work—is by pulling us into a vortex of endless information. It's like online dating.

Say you're on Tinder and the first thing you see are all these different guys. Lots and lots of guys, and you think to yourself: *Oh my gosh, there is so much choice. There are so many guys.* Then you start swiping. *Too old, too short, needs a job, needs a shave, too many tattoos (or not enough, if that's your thing)!*

Then you start talking to them to see who is a good fit, and the selection goes down, down, down even more. And you realize there isn't as much choice as it appeared at first.

The ads you see for entrepreneurial opportunities work the same way. While it can seem like there are limitless opportunities out there, too many are not nearly as profitable as they seem. And I have a unique vantage point to know this, being a behind-the-scenes advertiser who has run million-dollar launches and run launches that didn't go so well because it wasn't a desirable product or service, or didn't have enough proof that it really worked.

Let's apply a little bit of logic. There are a thousand choices, and they can't all be the best business to launch. But what is the one thing all these different businesses have in common?

They're all running ads

Wouldn't one of the best businesses of all be getting behind the engine that drives the entire platform? Un huh! And that's the online ads management business.

We get inundated with so many business venture choices that we can easily get overwhelmed—really overwhelmed. And the overwhelm can be a killer for productivity and progress in *just getting start-*

ed. Because then we start getting into analysis paralysis. We start consuming podcasts, reading articles, and reading the advertising. That's what I mean by the online labyrinth. It is disorienting, frustrating, and confusing. At some point you need to choose.

When it comes to making decisions, psychologists hypothesize that there are two types of individuals: the Maximizer and the Satisficer.

Maximizers want the very best for the long run. If a maximizer wants a blue blouse, she will shop for the best price, the highest-quality fabric, the best customer review, the fewest returns, and so on and so on. She will shop days and days to find it.

The Satisficer wants a blue blouse, sees one in the window of a shop she is walking past, walks in, tries it on, it fits, buys it, and goes to lunch. She is satisfied with her purchase that she has made rather quickly because it may not have been the perfect blouse, but it ticked the most important boxes.

The Maximizer has spent three days comparison-shopping before she makes a decision and chances are, she has buyer's remorse once she purchases the blouse, and second guesses if she has found the best possible option. *Will the price go down? Should I have chosen the one with the collar, or the pearl buttons? Maybe I should have gone with machine-washable instead of dry clean only?*

Barry Schwartz wrote a 2004 book about the frustration of decision-making when faced with too many choices, called *The Paradox of Choice*. We tend to think it is wonderful to live in a society where we have so many choices: 40 types of cereal, 20 types of toothpaste, but we are often struck with decision paralysis.

Is it any surprise that the Satisficers tend to be happier and more satisfied? The word "satisficer" is a combination of satisfied and suffice after all.

Schwartz tells us that the anxiety of too much choice is detrimental to our mental health. By limiting our choices, we can have a healthier and more satisfying life.

Yes, research is important, but it is also important to recognize that at some point, all that information is no longer a service, but a detriment because we can research stuff to death.

Bear in mind, the Facebook platform is designed to present us with as many options as possible because Facebook makes more money when we're continually consuming. At some point we just have to say, "You know what? This seems like a good idea. This makes sense. I'm going to take a leap of faith and I'm going to try this out." I suggest to people to just sit back and ask yourself: *What is my intuition telling me*? And then throw in some practicality.

Be a satisficer when choosing your business. One of the best pieces of business advice I ever got was from a coach who said, "Stop listening to everyone else and just listen to me for six months."

You can go off and consume stuff after that. But for right now, while you're birthing your business, put all your time, effort, dedication, and focus on *this* business to make *this one* work. The chances of success are going to be so much higher if you're able to drown out all those sounds.

This is something that I definitely tell the women that are in my program: "Just give me three months. Just listen to me and me only for three months. That way you're going to have a much higher chance of success." Don't get lost in the noise and in the online platform that just wants you to consume endlessly and never get any further ahead.

But what about passion?

I saw a TEDx Talk on the topic of passion and it completely changed my way of thinking. There are actually a couple of TEDx

Talks about passion being overrated. One is by Terri Trespicio who got laid off from Martha Stewart. She says, "Passion is not a plan. It's a feeling and feelings change."

Benjamin Todd spoke at TEDxYouth, and he gets right to the heart of the matter in the name of his talk: "To find work you love, don't follow your passion."

Suppose your passion is camping or painting. Does that mean you have to make a business out of it? No. Find a way that supports that passion. You don't necessarily want to ruin something you love by being forced to monetize it and "work it" seven days a week.

Passion is overrated

Just commit yourself to helping people and being of service to other people. And in a funny way, you will find your passion through that. Before I stumbled onto these TEDx Talks, while I was lost in the online labyrinth, I thought I should be following my passion. *Am I being a sell-out if I don't?* Then I realized, no, actually I'm not, because I just decided to get practical, help people, be of service, and fill a need in the marketplace because people are so confused about marketing businesses.

Sometimes your passion is making money

One of the biggest pain points is, *How do I market better? How do I get more people in the doors? How do I make more sales?* The online advertising world that drives these marketing needs is a huge place where you can provide immense service. By being practical, being of service to people, you can actually unravel your unrecognized passion.

For many women, their underlying passion is that they just want to feel like they're doing something meaningful and have a purpose in helping others.

Passion to business is what a soulmate is to your love life. We're misled with this idea that we've got to find our one soulmate in the world. I don't really think that exists. I think there are maybe 100 people in the world you could probably have a great relationship with. And it is the same way for business. By getting practical and wanting to make money on my own terms, I found my passion in an unexpected way: helping other businesses.

CHAPTER 11

A DAY IN THE LIFE

If you're curious about what it's like to be an ads manager, I'll talk a little bit about that now. The fun thing about being an ads manager is you don't do the same thing every day. When I worked for other people, I was expected to do pretty much the same thing day in and day out, and I am a person who needs variety to keep me interested.

The work can be creative; for instance, if you like writing, you can write your ads. If you don't like writing, you can pay someone to write the ads for you. An ads manager's day is a pretty even split of behind-the-desk work, client management, and speaking to potential clients.

As an ads manager, I wake up in the morning, enjoy my coffee and breakfast, and then do my daily exercise. Notice I said "enjoy" my coffee. That coffee tastes so much better from my favorite mug, sitting at my kitchen table, than it ever did when I bought a cardboard cup of it on the way into work.

Once the kids are off to school, I sit at my desk and plan my objectives for the day, which usually starts with checking in with my accounts to make sure all the ads are doing well. And that is quite simple; I log onto Facebook and see what the results look like.

On Mondays, I meet with current clients, which I find very enjoyable since it can be truly collaborative. I meet with clients by phone or Zoom every couple of weeks. Since I like the creative side, I will suggest the hook for their next marketing campaign on these calls and then write it later in the day. I have found that my best ideas come to me (like a lot of you) in the shower or while taking a walk.

Collaboration with clients is a lot of fun for me. I feel passionate about what we discuss. We're talking about marketing, we're talking about how we're going to make their business successful (or more successful). I like making money for my clients too because I know it means they can reach their goals and live their Why.

Tuesdays, Wednesdays, and Thursdays, I will spend maybe four hours on new client calls and no more than an hour of paperwork.

Fridays. A lot of ads managers don't even work full days on Fridays. Sometimes I will clean up a few loose ends so I can go into the weekend without that Monday morning dread.

You determine how many clients you want. If you want to work reduced hours, maintaining seven clients, you can definitely do that. Maybe you're driven to make $30K a month, have big goals and want to work full-time; then you can absolutely continue doing calls until you get your client roster up to that number of clients. You have a lot of flexibility with your schedule.

Want to go bigger?

You can scale your ads management business.

One person can handle about eight to 10 client accounts. On my own, I could handle a max capacity of about 10 clients. The way to scale is to hire someone to help you. You don't have to do it all alone and get burned out. Plus, when you are tired and stressed, you are not as creative and not as patient with the clients.

I started out by hiring someone who allowed me to go from nine or 10 clients up to 17. If you do the math on what each client pays you, around $2,000 a month, eight times $2,000, that's $16,000 a month. If you hire someone, even if you pay an experienced person a very generous salary of $60K a year, that's $5,000 a month that you would be paying that person. You would make $29,000 a month given you could handle an additional 7 clients.

For someone newer in the business, or someone who you feel has the potential if you train them, a salary of $40K a year is good. They can handle eight ad accounts. That means that you're paying them about $3,400 a month, and you're taking in $16,000 (8 ad accounts times $2,000 each = $16,000), minus $3,400 which equals a profit of $12,600). And over time, as you increase your reputation, $2,000 a month for your services is on the low end. Many of my ads management clients now pay my team $2,500 to $3,000 a month and more for my services.

Basically, you can run the agency yourself, managing your clients, or you can decide to hire a staff person and then you handle eight, they handle eight, and then again, if you want to go up even higher, you can hire another staff person to have two staff people, and they handle 16 clients, you handle eight, or maybe you just manage them. That's the way that you scale it.

I spend about one to two hours a day communicating with staff members and have tripled my client base and my revenue.

CHAPTER 12

WANTING YOU IS NICE, BUT NEEDING YOU IS BETTER

Facebook ad users are a highly profitable target market. Every business owner will want to work with you. It's one thing to learn a new skill; it's even better when people are willing to pay you for it. (And when I say Facebook, I also mean Instagram ads, as Facebook owns both platforms.)

When it comes to a business idea, it is best to start with something that is a need versus a want. One of my business mentors gave me this example: You want to sell a painkiller, not a vitamin.

What he means by that is, when you sell painkillers, people don't question the need for them. When you've gotten in an accident and you have surgery on your knee, you've got to take your painkillers. You literally will not be able to make it through the recovery without them.

I've got probably eight bottles of vitamins on my desk, and I haven't even taken one for three months because I just keep forgetting. I don't feel the need for one. But if I have a massive headache, you know I'll be motivated to take an Advil right now.

In business you can do one of two things. You can sell the painkillers, or you can sell the vitamins.

You can choose to hire a copywriter to rewrite all the copy on your website and they may or may not do a better job than you. This is not the same value or urgency as having someone running your ads and getting you more sales tomorrow. Now that's something people pay for, because it's a painkiller, not a vitamin. When you are assessing a business idea, you really want to be selling the painkiller, not the vitamin.

Savvy business owners know that if they hand over activities that others can do faster and better, that frees them up to perform functions that realize a higher return on investment (ROI).

For instance, let's say you spend two hours mowing your lawn every week. The college student who lives up the street says she will come by and do it for $30. You are a consultant who charges $175 an hour. In the time it takes you to mow the lawn, you could have billed $350. Doesn't it make sense to pay the college student $30 while you clear a profit of $310 without breaking a sweat?

A smart business owner knows she needs to advertise to get new customers. She *can* learn how to place her own ads but it's not the best use of her time. The first time someone places an ad, they can spend many days studying how to do it and still feel like they have no clue what they are doing. Then they invest $1,000 in the ads themselves. That's 20 hours they are not billing, revenue they are not collecting, and chances are they may get zero leads or sales from their first ad (unless you have had training, ads can be confusing).

When the business owner comes to you, they spend $2,000 for a month of skilled ad placement that drives customers through their door. Not only are they making money, but they are also reducing their stress levels. Instead of enduring one more learning curve, they can spend time on the aspects of their business they truly enjoy.

There are three categories of clients you can run ads for: lead generation, service-based, and e-commerce.

Lead generation

Lead generation is for local companies like: chiropractors, doctors, lawyers, mortgage brokers, real estate agents, insurance companies, car or body shops, restaurants, and many more. They need potential customers to contact them, call them up and ask about their service or walk into their store. They make the sale based on that contact.

Look in your town at all those types of businesses that need lead generation. Even your local gym, every single company you look at, they typically need to be running ads. Getting the work is not as hard as you might imagine. Open up an Excel sheet, or some kind of spreadsheet, list all the companies that you might want to run ads for, then go online and see who their competitor is, and see if their competitors are running ads.

Anyone can learn if a company is running ads just by going to their company Facebook page and looking at the page transparency section. Facebook will show if this company is running ads. Then you can look and see what ads they're running. If they're not running ads, go to their competitor.

Say you want to approach a chiropractor; go and see if there are any other chiropractors that are running local ads, and then you can either email, call, or walk in person to the chiropractor you are targeting and say, "I think you've got some potential because your competitors are running ads and you're not. I'd love to help you with some strategies."

Service-based businesses

People who are service-based are personalities, tutors, online entrepreneurs, and any type of consultant or coach. Life coaches, romance coaches, business coaches, and parenting coaches. Your ads can promote their courses, retreats, or hourly consultations. They are selling their time and expertise.

E-commerce

E-commerce is a very specific type of ads niche because they're selling products that can be ordered online: purses, candles, clothing, tools, food. Your ads drive people to their site instead of to their door.

You can use your own magic sauce and run your own ads. And that's what I teach the women to do in my program too, I show them exactly how to run their own ads to get people booking calls with them. That's the only way that I've ever gotten clients for myself. I've actually never done outreach. I just put up an ad and started from there.

B2B versus B2C

These terms may sound foreign to you if you're not in the business world. B2B means Business to Business. For instance, an auto parts manufacturer sells to auto repair shops and resale companies, not individuals. B2C means Business to Consumer. A bakery sells its cakes directly to the person who eats them. Some advertising clients will have B2C businesses, and some will have B2B businesses.

CHAPTER 13

ROI IS NOT A CAMPING STORE

ROI means "return on investment." This is a business term that means, "I put in a dollar and what do I get back?" Some business investments, you put in a dollar, and you lose money. When it comes to buying business services, many business owners only spend on what they really need (which makes sense)! Even if their website isn't perfectly written or designed, they think: *When I've got some extra money in the bank, I'll hire that copywriter to revamp all my website writing.* It often never happens. Looking at return on investment from a painkiller perspective is an essential ingredient for your business to succeed quickly. (This is not to say you cannot sell vitamins—it's just harder).

An ads manager offers a lot of strategy and interpretation of the market. Because of that, people really associate an ads manager with return on investment, because we have the math and facts to say, "We put together this campaign, we spent $1,000 and we made you $8,000." That's eight times the return on the work we did, and that's something that people will invest in again and again, because it's like an ATM machine—if you were to put in a dollar and get back eight (wait, isn't that more like a slot machine on a winning cycle?) It's a no-lose strategy, and why would you ever say no?

"What is the profit margin?"

So, this was me after being in business for so many years, failing at my first business, being a year into my ads management business, and I was just learning what the term "profit margin" means—and I don't consider myself a stupid person. Clearly, I sometimes tune stuff out that I don't need to know, but you need to know that some businesses have really poor profit margins.

Many brick and mortar companies consider 10% to15% profit margins really good! Whereas in my business, even working alone, your profit margins are going to be around 50%, meaning if someone pays you $2,000, you put a thousand in the bank.

When you start to hire people, your profit margin shrinks slightly, because you're paying a salary. The profit margins of an agency when you start to hire staff can become a little bit less, but even 30% to 40% profit margins are still exceptionally better than most brick-and-mortar businesses.

I attended a business event last year and there was a couple there boasting that their business made $2 million. Then on day two of the retreat, it came out that their profit margins were only 10%. That's $100K per person. Much less than the million-dollar business I initially thought they had.

It's important to also assess the profit margins of any business you consider starting. It is the difference between opening up a burger shop and saying, "Okay, I've got the burger joint. I've got the chairs, going to buy the fryers, hire a whole bunch of staff, and then cross my fingers and hope that my profit margins are 10%."

With a business like that, you're at the restaurant all the time. If you like that lifestyle, then by all means, if that's your passion, do it, because 10% may be enough to pay your bills. But if you've got bigger dreams and goals, that is not going to be the business that will make you a millionaire and give you the freedom to travel to Tahiti twice a year.

Worried about the competition? Don't be.

The figures below are what I present to my advertising students to illustrate that there is a healthy demand for ads managers.

To make $30K to $40K per month in the ads management business, you need 20 clients. That's a super healthy income, right? Let's think a moment: If 200 ads managers had 20 clients per month, they would be helping 4,000 businesses in total.

As of writing this book, there are roughly 31.7 million small businesses in the US[12]. In Canada there are 1.15 million small businesses[13]. This does NOT include medium or large businesses (and, yes! You can also help these.)

Let's say you want to make a million dollars. To make a million dollars you'd roughly need 100 clients—100 clients who stay with you a minimum of three months and invest $10K, which is the average minimum – not MAX but minimum!

If each one of them had 100 clients (let's say over a couple of years) and hit a million dollars, we'd collectively serve 20,000 business—20,000 businesses out of 32 million small businesses. That's 0.06%. This group of ads managers could double or triple in size and

[12] https://cdn.advocacy.sba.gov/wp-content/uploads/2020/11/05122043/Small-Business-FAQ-2020.pdf

[13] https://www.ic.gc.ca/eic/site/061.nsf/eng/h_03126.html

they'd still only be serving a very, very, small portion of the larger market. We don't even serve a drop in the bucket of all the businesses there are to serve, and would desperately benefit from our services.

Competition will not be a barrier in this business (yes, even today—right now). But your mindset about it could be.

CHAPTER 14

YOU DON'T NEED A KNIGHT IN SHINING ARMOR

When I was in my 20s, I hated budgeting and wasn't particularly driven to keep tabs on my money. One of my brothers told me I better marry rich because I was so bad with money. He assumed I would never be able to care for myself.

I'm ashamed to admit it, but for years I bought into that mindset. In fact, my mom frequently said, in a kind of joking way, that she hoped I'd marry a rich man who would take care of everything. My dad called it my knight in shining armor.

Know what? My "knight" never came. I always made slightly more than my boyfriends, because I'd gotten an advanced degree hoping I'd meet my knight in shining armor at university.

After my divorce, in my early 30s, I started dating in hopes I would finally have a chance to meet my knight in shining armor.

Never happened.

Now at 40 years old, I could not be happier that this knight never showed up in my life, because he could have never provided for me in the same way I've provided for myself. I now make more each month than I used to make per year, and I have the freedom and independence that comes along with that. Freedom is a benefit of money few people talk about without shame. The freedom is beyond rewarding.

The most obvious thing we overlook as a society when we condition our daughters to think they need a knight, is that a knight in shining armor comes with strings attached. I talk to women every week who must ask permission from their husbands to spend money, and that makes them feel suffocated. They badly want to start their dreams but feel stuck and unsupported and don't see a way out.

I know how drastically their lives would change if they had that independence they are craving. But we live in a society where women are shamed for wanting to marry into money, yet equally despised as unsexy or unattractive to men when they have money of their own, because they are considered too masculine!

There is a far better option: providing 100% completely and totally for yourself. And right now, with the accessibility and sheer volume of online information about business, this is totally possible. This is what drives me every day: to help other women have the very same freedom I have achieved.

I know many women who love helping people. Most people don't realize that when you're in the business of advertising and marketing, your whole day is helping people. You're helping business owners and you're helping reach and serve their clients, so it's very rewarding in that way.

We're sold the idea of "find your passion" in the same way we're sold the idea of "find your soulmate." The reality is there are multiple soulmates for us in the world, and there are also multiple passions.

A first step to getting started is to ask yourself these three questions:

- Do I like being creative?
- Do I want to live a different life?
- Do I love helping people?

Passion is important to leading a fulfilled life, but you don't have to wait to start a business until you find your passion. Making money and supporting yourself can be your passion.

No matter what business you decide to pursue, I hope that you now have a better understanding of the necessary ingredients you should consider before you invest in a program. To be successful you will definitely have to invest in getting the help you need to learn your craft. DIY-ing it is the fool's way of learning.

Even though I did invest a lot in my first business, I also DIY-ed the most important aspect of it, which was the marketing. The smartest business owners know that they need to invest upfront in learning how to do something. That's the difference between my first business and my second.

In my first business, I did a lot of it myself. Whereas in the second business, when I was back on the scene, I decided, *I'm making this business work, come hell or high water*. I paid someone to show me the exact business model she had, and I made that money back within six weeks.

That is proof that DIY-ing really is the fool's way of learning, and doing it all yourself can lead to extreme overwhelm. It can lead to things never happening. It can lead to you actually spending triple the amount of money you would have devoted to learning to run your business the right way (like I did!)

Look for a mentor who has the in-the-trenches experience, so you don't waste your money. A lot of the women who have come to me have said, "Oh, I've already worked with this program or that program. I don't believe any of it. It's all a scam."

And I say to them, "Well, what did you invest in?"

"Well, I invested in this affiliate product and then I realized I couldn't run Facebook ads and then my account got banned, and then I realized I'd wasted the $4,000."

Well, very sadly they invested in a program that was not a good business.

It's kind of a good news/bad news situation. It's good news because they could still crush it at another business (a good business idea like becoming an ads manager.) The bad news is, they've wasted a bit of money and have to start from scratch. But actually, even business failures come in really helpful in advertising, as did my raw food business. Even though I technically failed, I learned a lot.

I wrote this book to help women more quickly realize if they are meant for a business and for the entrepreneurial space. If you have felt unsatisfied with your life, I hope my story gives you permission to do what I did, and inspires you to go for it. Go for your dreams!

Even if you've already failed at a business or two or 20, **you can absolutely take all those business failures and turn them into a success** if you understand what went wrong before. Did you invest in the wrong type of business? If it's anything other than, "I didn't work hard," which is a crucial ingredient, then it means that it was probably the failure of the business, not you. If you were working hard at your business and your business didn't work, then it means you chose the wrong kind of business.

I wrote this book to show you the tools to understand what makes for a good business investment versus what doesn't make for a good business to start. I hope the information in this book will help you find your place, and give you the tools to start a profitable business.

Hopefully this information will help you become more passionate about the way you're living and raise the quality of your life, enabling you to spend more time with your family and do the stuff that makes you really excited. Take these tools and become your own business owner. It is a big shift in mindset—going from depending on someone else to provide a paycheck, to stepping into the mindset of an entrepreneur.

Here are three ways to get started if you want to learn more about becoming an ads manager:

- Attend my free "10K Months" training: https://watch.sarahmaeives.com/10kmonths
- Book a FREE call to speak with me (or one of my incredible program grads): https://book.sarahmaeives.com/questions
- If you have any questions or just want to say "hi!", please send an email to admin@sarahmaeives.com

Thank you, from the bottom of my heart, for reading my story.

Don't forget: All life involves risk. And a well-lived life involves taking measured risks that move you towards the life of your dreams.

Here's to wishing you the courage and faith you need to take those risks and move wholeheartedly in that direction.

May we not only live, but truly feel alive.

Sarah, xo

ACKNOWLEDGEMENTS

I am blessed to have the best family in the world. My mom is, and my dad and grandma were, my biggest cheerleaders and a huge part of my success. I am surrounded by the love and support of my children, Blue and Avigael; my mother, Cindy; my partner, Joachim; and my brothers, Jon, Will and Aaron (and Jared, in memory).

I want to thank all of the women who have worked with me, who have entrusted me to teach them. I celebrate all the hard, amazing work that they have done and appreciate everything that they offer to the program and to me. I always like to say as much as they learn from me, I have learned so much from them and it's such a rewarding path.

I want to thank my incredible team for being just as passionate as I am about helping as many women as possible start businesses of their dreams. Without my incredible team, I wouldn't be able to help nearly as many people as we have. And I feel like it's just getting started!

And finally, thanks to my business mentor Scott Oldford, for giving me the courage I needed to grow as an entrepreneur, plus the business geniuses I have had the pleasure of working with: Curt Maly, Cole Gordon, Cat Howell and my friends Jamie Contreras, Craig Bramall and Hakeem White. With their support and guidance, I have grown as an entrepreneur.